Front Cover Illustration:

People stand and stare at the once majestic City Hall, now in ruins.
Taken near City Hall Avenue looking north. — Edith Irvine photograph; James Irvine Collection

Two Weeks in San Francisco
The Story of the 1906 Earthquake and Fire

By

Douglas Westfall
&
Henry C. Koerper

Second Edition

The Paragon Agency, Publishers
Orange, California
© 2006

Two Weeks in San Francisco
The Story of the 1906 Earthquake and Fire

Westfall, Douglas   1949–
Koerper, Henry C. 1942–

Published by
The Paragon Agency
Orange, California
2006

1. San Francisco, Cal.
2. 1906 Earthquake and Fire
3. First Person Account
4. California History
   I. Title
   II. Authors

ISBN10: 1-891030-75-2   BWS
ISBN13: 978-1-891030-75-8   BWS
Library of Congress Control Number: 2006902902

Printed in the USA
2.5k, r2

Dedication

This book is dedicated to photographer Edith Irvine.

Growing up at Mokelumne Hill in the Sierra foothills gold country, Edith Irvine began a short-lived professional career in photography. When only a teenager, she was hired by what would become the Pacific Gas and Electric Company. She demonstrated her capabilities in a dramatic photo essay focused on the Electra Power Project, the first hydroelectric project in California.

Edith arrived in San Francisco by boat from Stockton just minutes after The Earthquake struck on April 18, 1906, at 5:12 a.m. She was well supplied with photographic equipment, and began several days of roaming The City capturing images of catastrophic events. The 5x7 glass plates were exposed during this adventure, when she was but 22 years of age.

The San Francisco plates, plus her Electra Collection, a Yosemite themed collection, and other materials came into the hands of her older brother's son, James Irvine. He later donated them as The Edith Irvine Collection to the Harold B. Lee Library Archives of the Brigham Young University Library.

The collection contains less than 300 images, for Edith abandoned serious photography sometime in the 1920s. She became a teacher, never married, and passed away in 1949.

The only known photograph of Edith Irvine as an adult.

Private Collection

Acknowledgments

The publisher would like to especially thank
James Irvine, Gina Janelli, and Darrell Colwell
for permission to use their photographic collections.
The James Irvine Collection is housed in the H. B. Lee Library,
at Brigham young University in Utah.

Each of these collections can be viewed and obtained:

James Irvine Collection — http://www.lib.byu.edu/historic_photos

Gina Janelli Collection — http://www.realimagepro.com/1906.asp

Darrell Colwell Collection — http://www.specialbooks.com/colwell.htm

Table of Contents

Preface

This remembrance of the 1906 San Francisco earthquake, conflagration, and subsequent dynamiting develops from a first person witness contained in correspondence from John Alphonso Cook, my grandfather, to his then fiancée, Mabel M. Moody, my grandmother. Had Mabel not traveled to Riverside for an April get-together with an older sister, Ida Moody Russel, instead of staying at the Moody home across the Bay, her beau "Al" would not have posted so detailed an accounting of the most horrific peacetime catastrophe of 20th century America.

California history is measurably richer for the legacy of the Cook-Moody letters, which my grandmother curated not merely because they were penned by her beloved "Allie," who preceded her in death by more than half a century, but also because she wisely anticipated that the missives would hold great import for future generations.

I knew my grandmother well, for she lived into her 98th year. However, I was just over two decades removed from acquaintance with my mother's father, who did not survive an overdose of ether during an appendectomy in 1921, when his daughter and only child, Barbara Jean, was but four years of age.

At the time of his demise, Al was employed as Head of the Remington Arms Metallic Cartridge Company in Portland and was roundly acknowledged as "one of the best known outdoor sportsmen in the West" and as a "famous trapshooter." Indeed, only three days prior to his passing, he was victorious in the Rose City Trapshooting Tournament (professional class) held at the Portland Gun Club. Al was also known as a "square shooter," a sobriquet unrelated to his sporting talents.

When my grandfather wrote the April 19 - May 2, 1906 letters, he was 24 years old, living with his mother, Luella, and sister, Henrietta, at 3924 19th Street, close to San Francisco's Mission District, and was working in The City for the Pacific Hardware and Steel Company. The year following, Al and Mabel took their nuptial vows. The unusual age differential, close to four years - the bride older - certainly raised a few eyebrows back then. But grandmother had already displayed an unconventional bent, having, for instance, graduated from a public high school at a time when few middle class girls attended coeducational secondary institutions. Parenthetically, one 1890s fellow student at Oakland High was the soon to be famous novelist and political activist, Jack London, whom grandmother disparaged as a "long haired ruffian" no self-respecting young lady would deign to give the time of day.

In 1912, the couple moved to Oregon when Al was promoted to manager of the Portland branch Sporting Goods Department of Pacific Hardware. In 1917, soon after a transfer back to San Francisco, my grandfather quit the company in order to assume a salesman position with Remington at their Seattle office. The return to the Pacific Northwest was especially memorable for the Cooks, for in tow was Barbara Jean, only recently adopted at birth.

In late 1919, Al Cook resigned from his sales job to become a partner in the Tacoma-based Kimball Gun Store, a wholesale and retail sporting goods firm, but disagreements precipitated by his partner's questionable business ethics made the association short-lived. The "straight shooter" was immediately rehired in 1920 by his previous employer, becoming the Head of the Remington Arms Company in Portland, remaining there until his untimely death the following year.

His widow soon returned to Oakland where her mother had only recently died. Shouldering a double loss and saddled with the sole support of herself and her young daughter, Mrs. Mabel Cook became a custom cake maker, operating out of her home. The business formula of this "renowned cake baker" was two-fold. Indubitably, she turned out an excellent product, but attuned to the climate of conspicuous consumption, cakes were priced high enough to offer customers a status symbol. When one wealthy epicurean queried another about ever having commissioned a "Mrs. Mabel Moody Cook cake," the subtext was whether that lady or gentleman could afford such an extravagance. At retirement, grandma's business counted a clientele of near a thousand.

Another Oaklandite, a Mr. Edy, who was as well known for his candy creations as Mabel was for cakes, had once proposed that she join him in a consortium of three confectioners. Mr. Edy, naturally, would manufacture the candy, grandmother would bake the cakes and cookies, and to produce ice cream, Mr. Edy was lining up a young fellow named Dreyer. Wearing her independent spirit on her sleeve as usual, Mabel politely declined, with the result that the consortium failed to materialize.

My grandmother, the kindly lady who frequently gifted me with Buffalo nickels gleaned from spare change, who introduced me to philately, numismatics, rock hounding and any number of other hobbies fascinating to a child, and who eventually entrusted me with the '06 Cook-Moody letters, passed away less than two years short of her 100th birthday celebration, an occasion for which she had anticipated baking a gigantic cake.

Henry C. Koerper, March 2006

Henry Koerper is primarily a prehistorian, retired from 35 years of teaching college level Anthropology. Dr. Koerper continues in the field of archaeology, working with Cultural Resource Management firms in southern California.

His primary research interests focus on the subsistence and settlement behavior of Native peoples who once lived in Los Angeles, Orange, and San Diego counties. He also studies the magical and religious practices of the region's various tribes.

He has over 75 journal publications on these and related subjects. Other publications have covered such diverse topics as ancient Greek numismatic art, American Indians in modern sports, and the local history of Orange County.

He is a member of many organizations including Sigma Xi, the American Anthropological Association, the Society for American Archaeology, and the Society for California Archaeology. He also serves on the board of the Pacific Coast Archaeological Society, in southern California.

Professor Koerper speaks at scientific meetings and promotes the field of archaeology by giving presentations at a variety of venues, including grade schools. This is his first book with The Paragon Agency, Publishers.

Foreword

Two Weeks In San Francisco came about through a friendship with coauthor Henry Koerper that sparked intense interest in the story of The 1906 Earthquake and Fire. His extensive collection of photographic and other material relating to the event is the keystone of this book.

Three professional photographers in 1906, one known and two anonymous, took collectively well over 100 glass plate photographs, most of which are published in this book. Darrell Colwell, who owned a photographic shop in the 1960s, had the opportunity to obtain 27 glass plate photographs of the '06 event. Gina Janelli received through her family, 35 glass plate photographs and the camera with which they were taken. Sadly, we know nothing about either of the photographers of these images.

A third photographer we do know. Edith Irvine took perhaps upward of 100 photographs of The Fire and Earthquake, yet until last year, only about 60 were known. I discovered five undocumented photos of Edith Irvine shortly before publishing this book. It is the combination of these three professional photographic collections and the personal letters of Dr. Koerper's grandfather that make this book a special contribution to the history of The Earthquake and Fire.

Douglas Westfall, April 2006

Douglas Westfall has been a publisher of American history for fifteen years and has had the opportunity to discover much new material relating to some of the really great stories of America. By publishing his own works, he maintains control over the quality and content of the narratives. Mr. Westfall also shares knowledge with the public through his lecture series on American History.

Gary Gabler Photo

In public lectures, the scholar often brings to light first person accounts collected throughout America. These include fascinating true life experiences from such subject areas as the Civil War, the sinking of the Titanic, and Amelia Earhart's flights. His lectures derive from the books he publishes through his company, The Paragon Agency. Douglas' books are sold on his website and at bookstores across the nation.

Mr. Westfall has delivered presentations throughout the United States, and in Canada, Latin America, the Philippines, and Europe. An educator, he has taught at the grade school through the community college levels.

Weekly, he offers free historical presentations at local grade schools. His research involves him with libraries, history centers, and universities. Douglas also chairs the Board of Trustees of the Orange Library and History Center and is actively involved in the curation and cataloging of the Library's history archives and extensive photography collection.

Introduction

The following book contains the first person account of a survivor of San Francisco's 1906 Earthquake and Fire. Sidebars are introduced to identify and describe important elements in his writing and within the text. The first chapter provides a historical background to show how this man, Al Cook, fits within his history. Much of the copy within the book comes from Cook's written account. The illustrations have references to sources, and an index provides cross references to elements of the story. This is the story of Two Weeks in San Francisco.

May 8, 1906 postmarked card from Al Cook to Mabel Moody, showing the collapsed Valencia Street Hotel. The message appears on the obverse of the postcard since postal regulations forbade anything but an address to be written on the reverse side, until 1907.

Postcard photograph taken from 19th Street looking north. — Private Collection

Post-1906, recently resurrected San Francisco with Treasure Island
and the Oakland Hills in the background.
Stereo photo taken from Twin Peaks looking east down Market Street. — Keystone View Co., Stereo

Chapter 1
The Turn of the Previous Century

This is a story focused on two weeks in the life of Al Cook during The City's 1906 Earthquake and Fire and the immediate aftermath. For almost all of those two weeks Al remained within the desolated metropolis. There he looked after his mother and sister, helped protect his workplace, and served people within his community.
— This is his story.

The turn of the previous century showed to the world the grand affluence of San Francisco. The great city lay upon the steep hills of its peninsula, covering the rolling landscape like a warm blanket. Seen from a distance at night, it was a bright and shining star, surrounded by the dark bay and the sea.

The sharp contrast is perhaps what gave the city its unique vibrancy. Vibrant as it was, San Franciscans simply called it The City. With a burgeoning population growing toward half a million, The City was the New York of the Pacific Coast. It was the financial center of California, the heart of western transportation, and a cultural haven for opera, theatre, and music. San Francisco was truly a modern city with gas, electricity, telephone, and telegraph services, plus it had a transportation system of boats, rail lines, and cable cars.

This cosmopolitan urban delight was at its peak, bankrolled by the great California Gold Rush and the Nevada Silver Boom a decade later. It was built up over layer upon layer of former burned-out buildings, sand-choked creeks, and the infilling of the bay. By 1900, San Francisco was barely a half-century old and yet was compared with the great cities of the world, including London and Paris.

There were problems in San Francisco with graft and corruption pandemic within The City. Every element of business and industry was affected, from shops on the street, to large construction projects — even City Hall.

The City erected upon the sand hills of this windblown peninsula was ripe for change. Change would come soon enough, without warning.

The San Francisco Peninsula.
Note the size of the Bay and the extensive creeks and swamp areas, later built up as landfill.
Laguna de los Dolores is in the lower left of the map.
Randall Chambers photo-art, after an 1853 U.S. Coast Survey Map of San Francisco. — Private Collection

Early San Francisco

Before there was a City of San Francisco, there was a fort, a mission with its pueblo, and a presidio, all established by the Spanish in 1776. The settlement came at a time when America was just getting to its feet, and the soldiers of the presidio were asked to volunteer a portion of their pay in support of the American patriots who were fighting the archenemy of Spain: Great Britain.

The Spanish fort, or *castillo*, was erected upon a headland, directly above where Fort Point now stands. During the early years, the bluff was sheared off to the waterline, and the brick fort was then constructed and served as a garrison during the Civil War. Years later, the Golden Gate Bridge was specifically engineered to curve gracefully over the historic fort, by then long unused.

The *Misión de Nuestro Sera Pico Padre San Francisco de Asís a la Laguna de los Dolores* was originally founded further east, near the Lake of Sorrows, *the Laguna de los Dolores*. Relocated uphill a few years later, Mission Dolores remains to this day. While the mission owned a vast majority of the headland, little was cultivated due to the weather and soil conditions.

It was the presidio however, that housed the first families of San Francisco. There were perhaps 50 soldiers, and the wives and children of those that were married lived within the confines of the walled presidio.

Spain lost its holdings in California when the people of New Spain revolted. By 1822, a

The painting of Mission Dolores is by Napoleon Primo Vallejo, General Vallejo's son and 16th child.
Private Collection

Mission Dolores

The historical record for the San Francisco area begins in 1769 when, from a distance, members of the Portolá overland expedition sighted the Bay. Several mariners had just missed discovering the Golden Gate and what lay inside.

Fernando Rivera y Moncada departed Monterey in 1774 seeking a suitable location for a mission and presidio. A major goal in establishing California missions was to address the welfare of Indians and convert them to Christianity. The mission system also functioned to serve the geopolitical goals of the Spanish Empire.

Father Junipero Serra had given the responsibility of founding Mission San Francisco de Asís to Fray Francisco Palóu who was attached to Rivera y Moncada's party. Although the Rivera y Moncada group reached the Golden Gate, the leader and Palóu rejected the area for settlement. In the following year, no mission or presidio sites were chosen when Palóu accompanied Bruno de Heceta, leader of yet another overland exploration party.

The next Spanish expedition, guided by Juan Bautista de Anza, arrived in San Francisco in 1776 and established the Presidio, which would provide protection for Mission San Francisco de Asís, which was founded at the same time.

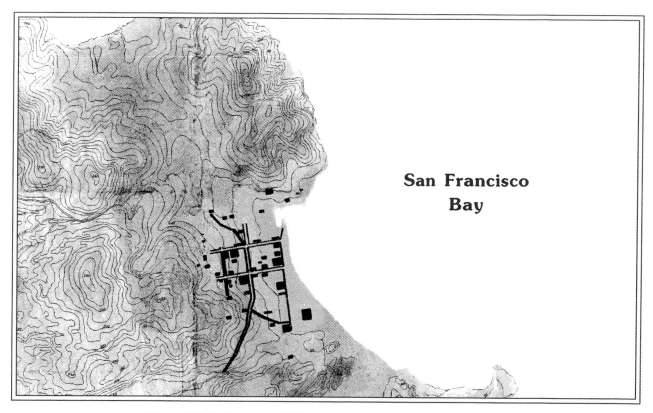

San Francisco
Bay

Town of Yerba Buena in 1847, just prior to the California Gold Rush.
Photo-art after an 1853 U.S. Coast Survey Map of San Francisco. — Private Collection

Presidio

The Presidio started life with a mere thirty-three leather jacket soldiers traveling with de Anza. The soldiers' duties were to defend the Mission, to protect the missionaries as they ventured forth into the wilderness, and to convey messages to and from Monterey. The Presidio de San Francisco was resupplied one or two times a year by packet ships sailing from San Blas, Mexico.

While mutually dependent, Mission authority and Presidio authority formed an uneasy relationship. Each had its own view of purpose on the frontier.

The Mission and Presidio came under the protection of Mexico as a result of Mexico's War of Independence. California became a province of Mexico in 1822.

new government lowered the flag of Spain, and raised the flag of the new republic of Mexico.

The early town came into being around 1834, when the Mexican government gave away the property of the mission to private individuals. Then called Yerba Buena, the entire village took up no more space than a few buildings around two city blocks, and the town grew slowly over the following 15 years. In Yerba Buena, Montgomery Street was on the shore, and the future Columbus Avenue was but a dirt track heading out toward the presidio. What later became Market Street was a trail winding its way up through the valley to the mission.

Massive California land grants were awarded at that time to those who asked for property. Over 800 grants were handed out in all of California over a period of only a dozen years.

The town of Yerba Buena then received the lion's share of the peninsula: 12,643 acres ranging from Vicente Street on the Pacific Coast to where Evans Street touches the bay. The last mayor, or *alcalde*, of San Francisco, José de Jesus Noe (Noah in the Bible), received the Rancho San Miguel, some 4,443 acres. Much of this is now Noe Valley, a district just south of the Mission. Noe's lands included all of what is now Mount Sutro, Twin Peaks, and Mount Davidson, with his holdings ending just south of the present-day city and county boundary.

The hostilities of the Mexican-American War came to an end in 1847, and California was added to the United States as a territory

Yerba Buena

As a result of the growth of cattle ranches in and around San Francisco and of trade in hides with Yankee ship captains, a busy port town, Yerba Buena, developed. In the course of the war with Mexico (1846-1848), United States forces captured Yerba Buena, and the port and town underwent a name change, becoming San Francisco. Now the Mission, Presidio, and Yerba Buena were in American control.

In 1847, no one could have imagined that within two years, the population would swell to some 5,000 souls. It would then range north and east from the present Castro Street at 22nd Street.

As San Francisco grew, so did the fire danger. Indeed, there were six devastating fires in the 1850s. In 1853, Henry Halleck constructed the first fire-proof building at the southwest corner of Montgomery and Washington. It survived The 1906 Earthquake and Fire, but it no longer exists.

Yerba Buena
From a Bosqui Eng Print of San Francisco in 1847.
Private Collection

A print of San Francisco in the 1860s.

Ray Co.

The Argonauts

Various travel strategies were employed by gold-seekers headed for the Mother Lode. The greatest number of argonauts ventured by prairie schooner, horseback, or simply by foot, usually along trails previously established by mountain men and early settlers.

The next greatest number of adventurers caught a ship to the Isthmus of Panama, and then by canoe, mule, and/or foot progressed to the Pacific side to wait for a clipper or steamer headed to California. Among their experiences were dysentery, cholera, malaria, yellow fever, and snake bites.

The most time-consuming trip, usually six months or more, was around Cape Horn. Seasickness and more serious maladies were common. Negotiating the Strait of Magellan was a terrifying experience, one that might last for days.

Often, sailors arrived at San Francisco jumped ship to head for the gold fields. This left hundreds of boats abandoned in the harbor.

the following year. The 1848 discovery of gold in the Sierra foothills brought masses of people, and in 1849 California's non-native Indian population swelled tenfold. Now, 50,000 people were swarming the Sierra Nevada; fully ten percent of that number was in San Francisco at any one time.

The Town of San Francisco

The village of Yerba Buena had now been renamed San Francisco, and construction began on a haphazard, if not grand, scale. The first photograph of San Francisco in 1850 shows hundreds of wooden buildings crowding the shoreline. These buildings didn't last long, as frequent fires burned them to the ground.

Ships in the harbor were deserted by the score, as gold-hungry sailors and passengers scrambled for the goldfields. These vessels were brought onshore, lashed together, and propped up with cut-down masts; these became stores, hotels, saloons, and brothels. They too burned to the ground or waterline when fires raged over the area. Covering the burned ships with sand, merchants would rebuild in place, moving the shoreline further out into the bay.

Opportunity had brought the less desirable elements of humanity. Thugs and gangs robbed and even killed local citizens. In the 1850s, some amount of vigilantism operated to curtail thievery, murder, and other criminal behavior, sometimes by hanging the worst offenders in public displays.

Multitudes of people came from all over the world into San Francisco, and they often brought more than just their luggage. Diseases raged throughout the tenements that were built along the wharves. Many people came via the Panama crossing, the way to avoid circumnavigating South America. So did malaria and a host of other ailments, much of which caused the demise of the poorer folk of The City.

The City of San Francisco

San Francisco had the largest natural harbor in the world at the time. Ships were at anchor by the hundreds, thereby creating a need for ever extending rows of piers. This created the Embarcadero, which reached from Potrero Point to around the headland, sometimes nearing 100 piers, wharves, and

Business Booming

On the eve of America's largest urban tragedy, The City's economic outlook brimmed with optimism. A building boom reflected the confidence.

As the 19th Century gave way to the 20th, a flurry of new construction was centered especially in the Financial District and along Market Street. The Flood Building at the corner of Market and Powell had just been completed, and now San Francisco could boast the largest office building in the West. Comstock Lode money was behind the edifice, as James Flood was one of the Nevada mining barons.

The Monadnock Building on Market and the Newman-Levinson and Whittell buildings near Union Square were soon to be finished, but work on the latter was not resumed for several years after the disaster. The Whittell Building was soon named the "Birdcage." On Powell Street, across from Union Square, a third wing was being added to the St. Francis Hotel. At the eastern edge of Nob Hill stood the massive Fairmont Hotel, almost finished and with its just completed interior. Times were good.

Whittell Building under construction.
Stereo View Co. - Stereo

This Central Pacific train, powered by dual locomotives, passes Chinese workers.
Frank Leslie's Illustrated Newspaper, 1878

Double unit cars of the California Street cable line at Central Avenue.
Ray Co.

docking areas.

The Butterfield Stage, the Pony Express —which ended at Sacramento — and the Central Pacific Railroad, all were part of San Francisco's early history. The first Butterfield Stage arrived in 1858, and the Pony Express mail, in 1860. The Transcontinental Railroad was completed in 1869.

Leland Stanford, Collis Huntington, and Mark Hopkins were Sacramento merchants who founded the Central Pacific Railroad (later joined by Charles Crocker). It was Theodore Judah, however, who proposed the idea of the railroad to Washington DC and President Abraham Lincoln. Congress passed the Pacific Railroad Bill in 1862, and Lincoln signed it, thereby starting railway construction during the American Civil War.

Justifiably so since Lincoln knew the United States desperately needed transportation to its Pacific states — where California gold and Nevada silver helped win the war for the Union. It was the "Big Four," Stanford, Crocker, Huntington, and Hopkins, who brought 15,000 Chinese workers to California to build the railroad. After the completion of the transcontinental railroad in 1869, these four men moved to the prestigious Nob Hill District of San Francisco, and some of the Chinese workers took up residence at the eastward face of that hill, called Chinatown.

Later on, the Silver Bonanza made four other men very wealthy. James Fair and John Mackay were miners, where William O'Brien and James Flood were bartenders. Going by

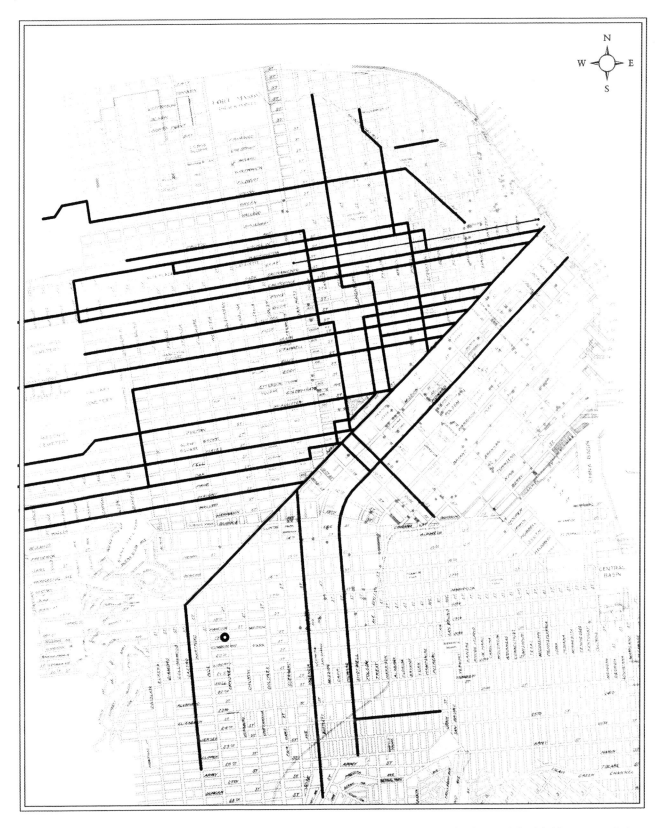

1906 Street Map of San Francisco, showing the maximum extension of the Cable Car lines. Al Cook's Home is circled.
Composite Map, Private Collection

Top: President Teddy Roosevelt receives a warm welcome from San Franciscans in 1903. At the time, San Francisco had many fellow Progressives. Roosevelt, among other activities, dedicated the Dewey Monument at Union Square (bottom) in an American self-celebration wrapped in the ideology of Manifest Destiny.

Both Private Collection

tips on the Washington Street Exchange in San Francisco, they invested heavily in the Nevada Comstock Lode when prices were low. Announcing their great silver strike of 1873, they each amassed a fortune of over $40 million — and also moved up to Nob Hill.

The Gold Rush had resulted in a population increase and great wealth, and the Silver Boom continued the rise of wealth in The City. The railroads brought even greater opulence and prosperity, along with myriads of people. It seemed that millionaires abounded on every corner, and opportunity was knocking on every door.

It was in 1873 that Andrew Smith Hallidie (actually his godfather's surname) built the first cable car line in San Francisco which ran from Portsmouth Square up Clay Street to Jones. It was but six blocks long, climbing a grade of nearly 10 percent. Within 25 years, nine different companies were operating cable cars for a distance of some 90 miles.

By 1900, however, three companies had reduced their lines, and one had gone out of business altogether: Hallidie's original line had lasted until 1899. With a fourth of its cable car miles shutting down, San Francisco was ripe for a new kind of local transportation. President Theodore Roosevelt, who came to San Francisco in 1903 for the dedication at Union Square, yet rode in a horse-drawn carriage.

With no bridges over the bay, steam-driven ferryboats criss-crossed the bay in seemingly every direction. The 1898 Beaux Arts Ferry Building, modeled after the clock tower of the Giralda Cathedral in Seville, Spain, reached a height of 245 feet. It was the transportation center of San Francisco until the Bay and Golden Gate bridges were built in the late 1930s.

The elegant grandeur of San Francisco on the eve of The 1906 Earthquake and Fire cannot be overemphasized. Its luxuriance and richness were almost beyond description. New fireproof buildings were going up everywhere, their iron skeletons first rising to the sky, then their concrete coats shrouding the offices and hotel rooms inside the multistoried structures. San Francisco was still on the rise as a new era was about to unfold.

Teddy Roosevelt's Visit to Union Square in 1903

Union Square is a pleasant park of palm trees and other ornamental vegetation set between the Financial District and the Theater District. The Square is but a short walk north of Market Street. The Square is bounded by Geary, Powell, Post and Stockton streets.

Its name derives from less pleasant times, recalling Civil War days when pro-Union, anti-Confederacy sympathies marshaled together hundreds and sometimes thousands of Lincoln's supporters onto that open ground for agitated demonstrations.

San Francisco, the grand spoils of the Mexican War, and looking west onto the vast markets of Asia, stood as the most logical metaphor of any American city for Manifest Destiny. Understandably, Teddy Roosevelt held a deep fondness for The City, and delighted in the warm reception received there, when in 1903, he dedicated a monument on Union Square to Admiral Dewey, commander of the Asiatic Squadron, and the "Hero of Manila."

The President's well-wishers were more than just fellow Progressives and Republicans, with whom some friction developed post-Earthquake and Fire, when T. R. acted decisively to squelch new outbreaks of anti-Asian sentiment.

The Dewey Monument is a 97 foot tall, granite Corinthian column, atop which is a bronze representation of Nike, or Winged Victory. Nike's face is modeled after a well known local benefactress, Mrs. Adolph de Bretteville Spreckels, wife of the "Sugar King." Emma Spreckels started her career as an artist's model, known for posing in the all together. She sought successfully to marry an older, very wealthy gentleman, unwittingly gifting Americans with a new term, "sugar daddy."

Private Collection

John Alphonso "Al" Cook

Al Cook was born in San Francisco on August 12, 1881. His father, Alphonso Maria Cook, married Al's mother, Luella Pease Cook, in Illinois in 1877. A daughter, Henrietta, was born after Al, also in The City.

At the time of the Earthquake and Fire, Al was living with his mother and sister at 3924 19th Street, in the Mission District. Al's father had passed away years before, and he was left to care for the family.

Al met Mabel Moody when both worked for the Pacific Hardware and Steel Company in San Francisco, and they became engaged. Al wrote to Mabel frequently during her spring visit to southern California, and he did so often throughout the 1906 disaster — the account used in this book.

Al Cook

John Alphonso Cook, 24 years old in 1906, lived in the Mission District in San Francisco with his mother and sister. Al was a sportsman and a member of the Wai Kai Kai Fraternity over on Guerero Street. He worked at Pacific Hardware and Steel down near the wharf, just a block from Market Street. Taking the Market Street Cable Railway from Castro, Al rode the three miles to and from work in relative comfort.

The Pacific Hardware and Steel Company had its general offices at Mission and Fremont streets. One warehouse was on Fremont, and two were on Main Street. The five-story office on Fremont was itself an imposing structure, but the warehouses covered nearly a city block each. With offices in other American cities, Pacific Hardware was a major contender in the business of hardware, iron, and steel.

Al lived on 19th Street, above the newly dedicated Dolores Park. The park covers two

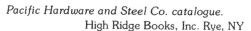

Pacific Hardware and Steel Co. catalogue.
High Ridge Books, Inc. Rye, NY

square blocks on a steep hill, just up Dolores Street from the mission. It had been created out of a former Jewish cemetery, after the headstones and bodies had been moved by a contractor. As public land became scarce, cemeteries were being removed to outside The City.

Next door to the mission was a large 1876 Victorian church, and across the street, Notre Dame Convent almost covered the entire block. The Mission District had grown during the Gold Rush, and the hillsides were now covered with homes.

From Al's home, the entire downtown could be seen. The house was built on a hillside, and his back window looked down Market Street toward the Financial District.

From Al's home was a panorama of grandeur and a view of Al's future — just what future would soon be evident by the next morning's events. The location of Al's home, the position of his employment, and his membership in his fraternal organization would dictate many of his actions.

Mabel Moody

Mabel Moody was a graduate of Oakland High School and unlike many young women of her day, was well qualified for her position, also at Pacific Hardware and Steel. She traveled daily on the ferry from her home in Oakland to San Francisco's downtown, where she met Al. Their courtship followed and then later the announcement of their engagement. Mabel was in Riverside, California, in April of 1906. She received Al's letters during the span of two

Mabel Emily Moody

Mabel Moody was born on Halloween Day, 1877, the fourth child of John Henry Moody and Mary Catherine Bunn Moody. Her father, a mechanic, had made two trips across the Plains to California by wagon and had at one time sought his fortune prospecting for gold. He married Mary Bunn sometime in the 1850s, and she joined him in San Francisco in 1868, after an arduous trip around Cape Horn with their 11 year old daughter, Ida.

The couple had four more daughters and finally a son, all born in San Francisco. Their second daughter, Martha Jane, died shortly before her fourth birthday. The family moved across the Bay in 1885, where Mabel attended Cole School and later Oakland High School.

Mabel fell in love with fellow employee John Alfonso Cook while working at the Pacific Hardware and Steel Company in San Francisco.

Private Collection

The New San Francisco Magazine — Private Collection

Mayor Eugene Schmitz

Eugene Schmitz was Mayor of San Francisco at the turn of the century. Tall, handsome, articulate and charismatic, Roman Catholic, a teetotaler, and family oriented, Eugene Schmitz projected the image of an upright political leader, but there was a dark side. In reality, he was a crook with crooked pals and was mentored by a crooked political boss, Abraham Ruef.

City government was dirty. The transportation and utilities companies regularly employed bribery to obtain city contracts. Southern Pacific exercised significant control in San Francisco, and almost certainly the railroad company added to the largesse received by the mayor, Boss Ruef, and members of the Board of Supervisors.

Reformers' efforts to root out bribery and graft were underway well before 1906. It is against this backdrop, this upwelling of potential disaster for Schmitz, that a different kind of disaster interceded, one that provided Schmitz a bright spot in a much soiled government career. The Mayor's finest hour was about to occur, in the heat of The Earthquake and Fire.

The New San Francisco Magazine — Private Collection

Brigadier General Frederick Funston

Not long after the turn of the century, San Francisco became home to Brigadier General Frederick Funston and his wife. Funston was a man of decisiveness and of action. This boldness was expected of a Medal of Honor recipient, one who had captured Aguinaldo, leader of the Filipino Insurrection. The General's heroic image was tarnished, however, by a reputation for vicious treatment of opponents in war, bullying of subordinates, and blatant self-promotion. Indeed, he drew the ire of the White House when on a cross-country speaking tour he promoted his strategy for "bayonet rule" in the Philippines. His outspokenness earned Funston exile to San Francisco to soldier under Major General Adolphus Greely.

Fate would intervene, however, and the General would once again be thrust into a high profile role in dangerous circumstances. Funston's upcoming part in the fight to save San Francisco could not occur without Greely's brief absence to participate in his daughter's Chicago wedding. The Major General was Pacific Division Commander, but now Funston was the ranking Army officer in The City on the eve of the temblor. He would soon stand center stage with Mayor Schmitz.

weeks beginning April 18th.

Schmitz and Funston

During San Francisco's 1906 Earthquake and Fire, the actions of two other men would also have a positive effect on The City and its citizens. These actions would be taken by Mayor Schmitz and General Funston.

The ability of these two men to take charge, organize, and move into action saved lives, reduced destruction, and brought order to the suffering metropolis. Each had the preparedness and the opportunity to meet with success, and each took advantage of that opportunity. From the mayor's proclamation to the general's orders to dynamite city blocks, their actions showed their prowess. Each of them however, had a much darker side than it would appear.

The City was at the top of its game and tomorrow would be even better it seemed, for San Franciscans had outlived vigilantes, epidemics, and numerous fires. Yet no one was ready for the great devastation that was to come on a spring morning in 1906.

San Francisco's numerous photographic studios catered to a wide range of clientele, with services generally affordable for middle class families. This charming 1906 pre-Earthquake and Fire image of three children, all in Buster Brown sartorial splendor, about to depart with baggage in a magnificent pedal car.
— Private Collection

Smoke billows above the Hotel Manhattan and the Studebaker Bros. warehouse, both located on the upper end of Market Street. A man carries a bundle toward the French Laundry wagon, as other people mill about.
Taken from Valencia Street looking northeast toward Market Street. — Edith Irvine photograph; James Irvine Collection

Chapter 2
Earthquake, Fire & Dynamite

"I pray to God I may never see such wreck and ruin again. People are lying dead in the streets, burned to a crisp. The whole downtown district is in ruins from Valencia Street to the bay. Everything on the hill [Nob Hill] is gone." - Al Cook

The San Francisco Earthquake was the seventh largest in the recorded history of the contiguous United States, and the 19th largest in the recorded history of the world. Now rated at 7.8 on the modern Richter Scale, the measurement of the times rated it a nine out of ten.

Over 200,000 people were left homeless, 28,000 buildings were destroyed, and four square miles of the city — from Van Ness to the bay — were burned to the ground. The Earthquake and Fire caused an estimated loss of $500 million. Equivalent to today, San Franciscans suffered $10 billion in losses. Beside the damage by earthquake and fire, the dynamiting for firebreaks reduced many buildings to rubble.

Out of a municipality of well over 400,000 people, some 3,000 people died, although accounts at the time quoted less than 500 perished. First accounts showed only 260 deaths, and following contemporary accounts brought the number up to 460. Obviously, some were not earthquake, fire, or dynamite related, and the causes of death happened for many reasons.

The earthquake occured during the early morning in San Francisco. On Wednesday, April 18th, dawn had not yet fully lit the streets, although some lamps were already going out. Cats ran and hid, and dogs barked in muffled tones. Horses working their early morning shifts became unsettled in the quiet of daybreak. The Produce District had started to set up, and ferryboats waited in the bay for first light to be able to dock.

The violent shudder of the earthquake at 5:12 am was something no living person had

An as yet unused steam pumper fire engine sits in a residential area.
Taken from an unidentified location. — Edith Irvine photograph; James Irvine Collection

Firefighters spray a burning building.
Ray Co.

ever experienced, at least at that level of intensity and inside a city. Buildings fell in on themselves, and streets caved into the ground. Collapsed masonry was everywhere, although many structures survived with little apparent damage. Dozens of fires started up, and the numerous companies of the Fire Department raced to the different districts. Some 500 firemen were now working feverishly, with but only 50 fire wagons to fight more than 50 fires.

The many citizens of San Francisco who were not already up and awake were awakened now. Many of those who were not injured went immediately outside to see all that had happened; many others found their doors had jammed, and they were now trapped.

The clock on the Ferry Building stopped at 5:13 when the earthquake unsettled the sleeping city. It had hit a minute before, without warning. In a matter of moments, buildings were downed and destroyed, as fires started up in The City.

The San Francisco Fire Department was severely hampered by several developments. At the start of the earthquake, the fire chief lay dying on the bottom floor of the city's main fire station. The adjacent building had fallen onto his second-floor room carrying him and his wife to the bottom floor. All the glass-cased fire alarm batteries were upended and useless, and all three water mains were crushed underneath the streets. The only continuously working fire hydrant within the entire city was up in the Mission District, above Dolores Park.

There was water however in a saltwater line that ran down Market Street, and there were up to 16 city cisterns located throughout The City, from Telegraph Hill to South of the Slot. Additionally, there were three cisterns in the Mission District. Yet these went largely untapped throughout the day.

Also, there were private cisterns under permanent buildings — essentially privately owned fire systems, which after their discoveries, were used to fight fires. The Palace Hotel itself was in the process of extinguishing its fires with its own water system, when firemen in the street tapped into

Company "L" Millitia from Santa Ana, Calif., assembled to deal with the many refugees. Taken from an unknown location. — Private Collection

Authority Maintained

The epicenter of first response to The Earthquake was the Hall of Justice on Kearny Street. Mayor Schmitz had rejected City Hall on survey of its helpless condition. Just across the street from Portsmouth Square, the Hall of Justice was itself in poor shape, its roof and tower collapsed, and it held 82 very nervous prisoners, their cell's bars torqued and locks twisted. With some difficulty, the prisoners were released from their potential death traps and sent either to Alcatraz Island or escorted by the militia to Fort Mason, depending on the seriousness of their crimes.

Meeting his police commissioners, the Mayor first ordered all saloons to shut down. Next, this group compiled names of fifty prominent men to sit on a "Committee of Safety," soon to be chaired by an ex-mayor, James D. Phelan.

Assembling at Portsmouth Square and subsequently retreating to the brand new Fairmont Hotel on Nob Hill, the Committee members distanced themselves from the approaching inferno. Left behind at the Square were corpses from the morgue and bodies only recently collected by the Coroner's Office. The dead were quickly given shallow interment. As the flames drew near, salvaged records from the Hall of Justice also had to be left behind in the Square, hidden beneath wet blankets.

Broken cable car tracks on Union Street.
Underwood & Underwood Publishers - Stereo

their water supply and diverted it to other blazes. The result was the incineration of the Palace Hotel.

Every cable car line was disrupted. Tracks were bent, underground cables were badly twisted, many not even underground anymore. All but two of the powerhouses were gone, and of the numerous cable cars operating, all had stopped. All of this and more had happened by 5:15 am.

Buildings were destroyed for some 100 miles, both north and south of The City. Other cities in northern California were damaged by the earthquake, yet were not burned. Around 10 a.m. that day, Los Angeles — some 400 miles south — experienced two earthquakes while its citizens were waiting to hear news of the fate of San Francisco.

On 19th Street, up in the Mission District, Al Cook was awakened by the jolt. From his window, he could see all of downtown.

Pass to the burned area signed by Police Chief Denan.
Mission Dolores Collection

San Francisco, April 22, 1906

TO ALL CIVIL AND MILITARY AUTHORITIES:

Pass bearer through the lines.

Chief of Police

The smallest of the three houses has suffered the worst indignity, having been knocked off its foundation.
Taken from Howard Street near 17th looking east. — Gina Janelli Collection

Interior of the Masonic Temple.
Stereo View Co. - Stereo

Claus Spreckels home on Van Ness Avenue.
Stereo View Co. - Stereo

Top: *Structural damage is evident to the buildings on the right side of the street, as the street has shifted vertically.*
Bottom: *Little earthquake damage is visible, although a part of an advertisement has tumbled from its perch.*
Both taken from unknown locations. — Gina Janelli Collection

Top: Significant structural damage to tenements; the sign says "For Rent."
Bottom: Serious damage to the Abramson-Heunisch Glass Company.
Top: Taken on Sutter Street near Market. Bottom: Taken on Market Street at Main. — Gina Janelli Collection

A boy glances at the camera as men lift water out of a fissure near the Valencia Street Hotel.
Taken on Valencia Street from 19th looking north. — Edith Irvine photograph; James Irvine Collection

Post Office entrance on Mission Street.
Stereo View Co. - Stereo

John Alphonso Cook
Wednesday, Day 1 (18th)
Mission District, San Francisco

Just after the shock, I went down to Valencia Street and worked for two and a half hours on the Valencia Street Hotel. The hotel was a four story frame building and went down in a heap, burying about 100 people. The earth is split open, and it has sunk about ten feet. Stores are all knocked topsy-turvy, and in a great many cases, you cannot see them at all as they have sunk out of sight. The tracks on Valencia Street are like the letter S, and the whole street is twisted.

As I was saying, I worked on the Valencia Street Hotel, and we chopped out dozens of people, some dead and some alive. I had the pleasure of saving a whole family: a mother & father and a little baby girl. I was poking around with my ax, calling, and I heard the woman answer. I chopped through the wreckage, and after some hard work, managed to locate them.

The mother called to save her child, and as luck would have it, I soon had the little one safe and sound. The dear little baby was nursing a rubber nipple and was not even scratched. The mother was not hurt, and it was worth any amount of labor to see the joy of that mother at having her baby restored

Valencia Street Hotel shown collapsed. This colorized postcard printed in Germany and sent to Mabel by Al Cook in 1908. Taken from 19th Street on Valencia looking north. — Private Collection

The Valencia Street Hotel

The Valencia Street Hotel has the dubious distinction of being the site of the single largest number of fatalities. The tragedy may have never occurred had the building not been constructed on a drained lake, consolidated with fill material. The lower three stories of the Valencia Street Hotel, actually a boarding house, sank and pancaked into the ground, with the fourth story coming to rest relatively intact at street level atop the others.

From only half a mile away, to the west, Al crossed Dolores Park, Dolores Street and Guerrero to reach the hotel on Valencia Street. Another cool-headed rescuer was former Mayor James Phelan, whose residence stood a mere furlong due north of the Valencia, that is until it was consumed by fire.

The baby girl Al freed and lifted from the rubble unscathed was the granddaughter of the hotel's owner, whose body was never recovered. The child's grandmother and mother survived unharmed, but the child's father was injured. Sadly, an uncle was one of the approximately 50 to 100 residents who perished, either crushed to death in the collapse or drowned below the street.

Top: The temblor stripped the walls from upper rooms of the Pierce-Rudolph Storage Company.
Bottom: Two adults stand by a collapsed house while a small boy gazes at a photographer.
Top: Photograph taken from Grove Street toward Buchanan. Bottom: Taken at Steiner and Pacific Avenue. — Gina Janelli Collection

Sharon Quarters for Children with much of its roof collapsed at the Children's Playground in Golden Gate Park.
Taken from the carousel looking northwest. — Gina Janelli Collection

to her safe and sound. The man was held down by a plank which was across his foot, but he was not badly injured. The only thing that saved them was that they slept in iron bedsteads.

You cannot imagine the suffering which has been caused by the trembler. People are dead by the score, and on top of it all the whole city is slowly burning up. The water mains are broken, and in consequence there is little or no water with which to fight the fire. We thank God, with all our hearts, that my Mother, Sister and myself are safe and in good health.

People taking refuge on the docks during the fire.
Clinton Johnson - Stereo

Dense smoke in the distance, seen across the rooftops of homes just below Nob Hill. The Call Building is towards the right.
Taken from Nob Hill looking southeast. — Edith Irvine photograph; James Irvine Collection

Market Street devastation.
Stereo View Co. - Stereo

Thursday, Day 2 (19th)

The whole downtown district is in ruins from Valencia Street to the bay, and the fire is now raging on the Powell Street hill, and is now burning the Fairmont and Hopkins. Everything on the hill is gone. The Saint Francis went about 2:00 am this morning; the Call burned yesterday noon. Can you imagine, the city is nothing but ruins.

The town is under martial law, and the soldiers are taking all provisions and dealing them out evenly to those who most need them. The suffering is terrible.

The Call Newspaper

The 18-story Call Newspaper, also known as the Claus Spreckels Building, is igniting one floor at a time, top-down on the afternoon of April 18th. Oxygen was sucked through the elevator shaft and fueled the inferno. The immediate area was known as Newspaper Row, and the Bulletin, Chronicle, and Examiner were all put out of commission.
Taken from O'Farrell Street toward Third and Market looking east. — International Stereograph Co. - Stereo

The Call=Chronicle=Examiner

SAN FRANCISCO, THURSDAY, APRIL 19, 1906.

EARTHQUAKE AND FIRE: SAN FRANCISCO IN RUINS

DEATH AND DESTRUCTION HAVE BEEN THE FATE OF SAN FRANCISCO. SHAKEN BY A TEMBLOR AT 5:13 O'CLOCK YESTERDAY MORNING, THE SHOCK LASTING 48 SECONDS, AND SCOURGED BY FLAMES THAT RAGED DIAMETRICALLY IN ALL DIRECTIONS, THE CITY IS A MASS OF SMOULDERING RUINS. AT SIX O'CLOCK LAST EVENING THE FLAMES SEEMINGLY PLAYING WITH INCREASED VIGOR, THREATENED TO DESTROY SUCH SECTIONS AS THEIR FURY HAD SPARED DURING THE EARLIER PORTION OF THE DAY. BUILDING THEIR PATH IN A TRIANGUAR CIRCUIT FROM THE START IN THE EARLY MORNING, THEY JOCKEYED AS THE DAY WANED, LEFT THE BUSINESS SECTION, WHICH THEY HAD ENTIRELY DEVASTATED, AND SKIPPED IN A DOZEN DIRECTIONS TO THE RESIDENCE PORTIONS. AS NIGHT FELL THEY HAD MADE THEIR WAY OVER INTO THE NORTH BEACH SECTION AND SPRINGING ANEW TO THE SOUTH THEY REACHED OUT ALONG THE SHIPPING SECTION DOWN THE BAY SHORE, OVER THE HILLS AND ACROSS TOWARD THIRD AND TOWNSEND STREETS. WAREHOUSES, WHOLESALE HOUSES AND MANUFACTURING CONCERNS FELL IN THEIR PATH. THIS COMPLETED THE DESTRUCTION OF THE ENTIRE DISTRICT KNOWN AS THE "SOUTH OF MARKET STREET." HOW FAR THEY ARE REACHING TO THE SOUTH ACROSS THE CHANNEL CANNOT BE TOLD AS THIS PART OF THE CITY IS SHUT OFF FROM SAN FRANCISCO PAPERS.

AFTER DARKNESS, THOUSANDS OF THE HOMELESS WERE MAKING THEIR WAY WITH THEIR BLANKETS AND SCANT PROVISIONS TO GOLDEN GATE PARK AND THE BEACH TO FIND SHELTER. THOSE IN THE HOMES ON THE HILLS JUST NORTH OF THE HAYES VALLEY WRECKED SECTION PILED THEIR BELONGINGS IN THE STREETS AND EXPRESS WAGONS AND AUTOMOBILES WERE HAULING THE THINGS AWAY TO THE SPARSELY SETTLED REGIONS. EVERYBODY IN SAN FRANCISCO IS PREPARED TO LEAVE THE CITY, FOR THE BELIEF IS FIRM THAT SAN FRANCISCO WILL BE TOTALLY DESTROYED.

DOWNTOWN EVERYTHING IS RUIN. NOT A BUSINESS HOUSE STANDS. THEATRES ARE CRUMBLED INTO HEAPS. FACTORIES AND COMMISSION HOUSES LIE SMOULDERING ON THEIR FORMER SITES. ALL OF THE NEWSPAPER PLANTS HAVE BEEN RENDERED USELESS, THE "CALL" AND THE "EXAMINER" BUILDINGS, EXCLUDING THE "CALL'S" EDITORIAL ROOMS ON STEVENSON STREET BEING ENTIRELY DESTROYED.

IT IS ESTIMATED THAT THE LOSS IN SAN FRANCISCO WILL REACH FROM $150,000,000 TO $200,000,000. THESE FIGURES ARE IN THE ROUGH AND NOTHING CAN BE TOLD UNTIL PARTIAL ACCOUNTING IS TAKEN.

ON EVERY SIDE THERE WAS DEATH AND SUFFERING YESTERDAY. HUNDREDS WERE INJURED, EITHER BURNED, CRUSHED OR STRUCK BY FALLING PIECES FROM THE BUILDINGS, AND ONE OF TEN DIED WHILE ON THE OPERATING TABLE AT MECHANICS' PAVILION, IMPROVISED AS A HOSPITAL FOR THE COMFORT AND CARE OF 300 OF THE INJURED. THE NUMBER OF DEAD IS NOT KNOWN BUT IT IS ESTIMATED THAT AT LEAST 500 MET THEIR DEATH IN THE HORROR.

AT NINE O'CLOCK, UNDER A SPECIAL MESSAGE FROM PRESIDENT ROOSEVELT, THE CITY WAS PLACED UNDER MARTIAL LAW. HUNDREDS OF TROOPS PATROLLED THE STREETS AND DROVE THE CROWDS BACK, WHILE HUNDREDS MORE WERE SET AT WORK ASSISTING THE FIRE AND POLICE DEPARTMENTS. THE STRICTEST ORDERS WERE ISSUED, AND IN TRUE MILITARY SPIRIT THE SOLDIERS OBEYED. DURING THE AFTERNOON THREE THIEVES MET THEIR DEATH BY RIFLE BULLETS WHILE AT WORK IN THE RUINS. THE CURIOUS WERE DRIVEN BACK AT THE BREASTS OF THE HORSES THAT THE CAVALRYMEN RODE AND ALL THE CROWDS WERE FORCED FROM THE LEVEL DISTRICT TO THE HILLY SECTION BEYOND TO THE NORTH

THE WATER SUPPLY WAS ENTIRELY CUT OFF, AND MAY BE IT WAS JUST AS WELL, FOR THE LINES OF FIRE DEPARTMENT WOULD HAVE BEEN ABSOLUTELY USELESS AT ANY STAGE. ASSISTANT CHIEF DOUGHERTY SUPERVISED THE WORK OF HIS MEN AND EARLY IN THE MORNING IT WAS SEEN THAT THE ONLY POSSIBLE CHANCE TO SAVE THE CITY LAY IN EFFORT TO CHECK THE FLAMES BY THE USE OF DYNAMITE. DURING THE DAY A BLAST COULD BE HEARD IN ANY SECTION AT INTERVALS OF ONLY A FEW MINUTES, AND BUILDINGS NOT DESTROYED BY FIRE WERE BLOWN TO ATOMS. BUT THROUGH THE GAPS MADE THE FLAMES JUMPED AND ALTHOUGH THE FAILURES OF THE HEROIC EFFORTS OF THE POLICE FIREMEN AND SOLDIERS WERE AT TIMES SICKENING, THE WORK WAS CONTINUED WITH A DESPERATION THAT WILL LIVE AS ONE OF THE FEATURES OF THE TERRIBLE DISASTER. MEN WORKED LIKE FIENDS TO COMBAT THE LAUGHING, ROARING, ONRUSHING FIRE DEMON.

NO HOPE LEFT FOR SAFETY OF ANY BUILDINGS

San Francisco seems doomed to entire destruction. With a lapse in the raging of the flames just before dark, the hope was raised that with the use of the tons of dynamite the course of the fire might be checked and confined to the triangular sections it had cut out for its path. But on the Barbary Coast the fire broke out anew and as night closed in the flames were eating their way into parts untouched in their ravages during the day. To the south and the north they spread; down to the docks and out into the resident section, in and to the north of Hayes Valley. By six o'clock practically all of St. Ignatius' great buildings were no more. They had been leveled to the fiery heap that marked what was once the metropolis of the West.

The first of the big structures to go to ruin was the Call Building, the famous skyscraper. At eleven o'clock the big 18-story building was a furnace. Flames leaped from every window and shot skyward from the circular windows in the dome. In less than two hours nothing remained but the tall skeleton.

By five o'clock the Palace Hotel was in ruins. The old hostelry, famous the world over, withstood the seige until the last and although dynamite was used in frequent blasts to drive

Continued on Page Two

BLOW BUILDINGS UP TO CHECK FLAMES

The dynamiting of buildings in the track of the fire, to stay the progress of the flames, was in charge of John Bermingham, Jr., superintendent of the California Powder Works. Several experienced men from the powder works, assisted by policemen and members of the fire department, did the hazardous work of blowing up the buildings. They were razed in sets of threes, but the open spaces where the shattered buildings fell were quickly turned into holocausts of flame. The work was most effective in the business blocks east of Kearny street.

WHOLE CITY IS ABLAZE

At 10 o'clock last night the Occidental Hotel was destroyed by the flames which swept unchecked across Montgomery street and attacked the block bounded by Montgomery, Sutter, Bush and Kearny. The new Merchants' Exchange building was a mass of flames from basement to tower.

The Union Trust building and Crocker-Walworth Bank were both ablaze and the Chronicle building and other buildings in that block were threatened by the flames.

Shortly after 10 o'clock the fire had eaten its way southward from Portsmouth Square to Kearny and California streets. The entire section fronting the west side of Kearny street seemed doomed.

All the building adjoining the Hall of Justice were ablaze and the firemen were striving to save the structure by using dynamite. It is almost a certainty that every building contained in the section bounded by Clay, Kearny, Market and East streets will be consumed.

The flames had eaten their way westward into the residence section as far as Gough street. There, by dynamiting blocks after blocks, the firemen succeeded in checking the devouring element.

CHURCH OF SAINT IGNATIUS IS DESTROYED

The magnificent church and College of St. Ignatius, on the northwest corner of Van Ness avenue and Hayes street represents in its destruction a material loss of over $1,000,000. The actual cost of the great building was over $900,000, but during the years which have elapsed since its erection the church has been enriched by paintings and frescoes, which were priceless. Some of them were works of art which can never be replaced, however willing those interested in the church might be to meet any expense in the effort.

MAYOR CONFERS WITH MILITARY AND CITIZENS

At 1 o'clock yesterday afternoon 50 representative citizens of San Francisco met the Mayor, the Chief of Police and the United States Military authorities in the police office in the basement of the Hall of Justice. They had been summoned thither by Mayor Schmitz early in the forenoon, the fearful possibilities of the situation having forced themselves upon him immediately after the shock of earthquake in the morning, and the news which at once reached him of the completeness of the disaster. He lost no time in making out a list of citizens from whom to seek advice and assistance, and in summoning them to the conference. It was called at the Hall of Justice, as virtually the first news which reached the Mayor regarding the extent of the disaster was that of the ruin of the City Hall. He did not realize that even while the conference was to be going on cornices would be crashing down and windows falling in fragments in the Hall of Justice also, and that before sunset desperate efforts would be made to blow the structure up in the vain endeavor by this means to check the advance of the flames in the northern section of the downtown district.

All, or nearly all of the citizens summoned to the conference

Continued on Page Two

Call-Chronicle-Examiner Newspaper

A most unusual news publishing event occurred on April 19, 1906. On Wednesday evening, three rival San Francisco newspapers, their buildings near each other on Newspaper Row and all on fire, agreed to join forces in putting out a free newspaper. Using facilities belonging to the *Oakland Tribune* an edition of 40,000 copies was printed. A quarter of the copies were circulated in San Francisco and a quarter in Oakland; the rest were distributed in other cities. Understandably, there were factual inaccuracies, such as the story on the front page asserting that President Roosevelt had declared martial law.

It was a coincidence that the name of this one-shot paper, a combination of the names of all three, "Call-Chronicle-Examiner," reversed the order of the competitors by circulation numbers. However, the Call with its smallest circulation held bragging rights to the tallest building in San Francisco.

The Call Building, also known as the Claus Spreckel's Building, stood 18 stories high, and with its dome it reached over 300 feet. It was The City's first skyscraper. The interior burned, but the basic structure remained intact, a circumstance that gave the building an eerie glow in many photographs of the Call on fire. The Hearst Building was just across the street at Market and Third Streets. The fire department and Army worked together to dynamite the home of the Examiner. The de Young Building, which housed the Chronicle, burned fiercely at the corner of Kearny and Market Streets, near Lotta's Fountain. It had suffered severe damage when Linotype machines toppled and crashed through the floors with the temblor.

Left:
The cover page of the Call-Chronicle-Examiner, *printed as a combined newspaper on April 19, 1906.*
Taken from an original copy.
Private Collection

Right:
The Call Building at right after The Fire. Hearst Building housing the Examiner Newspaper *is at the left.*
Taken on Market Street looking east.
Stere View Co. - Stereo

Pacific Hardware & Steel

The Fremont Street office of Pacific Hardware had two vice presidents, a treasurer, plus a Travelers' Department, Export Department, and a Foreign Department. It also contained Buyers, Shipping, and Order Departments as well.

Their warehouses contained builders hardware of all kinds: hinges, furniture handles, locks, and bolts. Also, they carried household goods: pots, pans, rat traps, toasters, bone and coffee mills, ice cream freezers, and sewing machines. Then there were sporting goods: pocket knives, rifles, handguns, fishing tackle and more.

The Main Street warehouses held only iron works and steel for use in the construction trade. Business was booming in San Francisco for Pacific Hardware.

Their catalogue was a thousand pages thick, and the company shipped their products worldwide. All their hardware would find use in The City, very, very soon.

Pacific Hardware and Steel Co. main office, located on Fremont Street at Mission Street, and the Beale Street iron warehouse just behind.

Pacific Hardware letterhead — Private Collection

The sight of the burning city is truly grand, yet it is awful when you think of the loss of property and life. I do not know what we will do. There is no place to buy things, and they will not allow a fire to be built in any home. People are cooking on camp stoves and over fires of every description. We are fine as we have a tent and a camp stove. We had fried eggs and flapjacks for breakfast.

I went down to the store this morning, and I pray to God I may never see such wreck and ruin again. People are lying dead in the streets burned to a crisp. The suffering amongst the poorer class who lived in that district will be terrible as in a great many cases all they saved was the clothes they wore.

The Pacific Hardware and Steel is not burned, and we will resume work in a few days. It is the only store of any size left in the City. Some of the outside walls were shaken down, and the two tanks went through the building, from roof to basement. The buildings were not otherwise damaged,

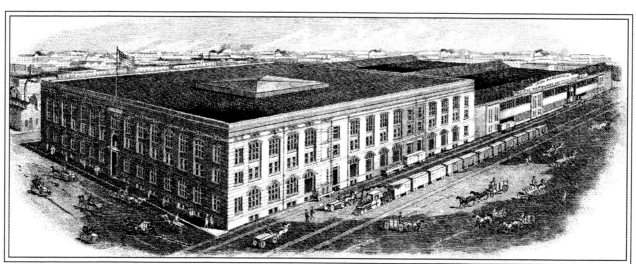

Cable cars are stalled on their tracks in the path of the inferno moving up California Street.
Onlookers sit on their only belongings as the fire moves uphill.
Two sequence photographs taken on California Street looking east. — Edith Irvine photographs; James Irvine Collection

A vortex of smoke in the background suggests a firestorm near the R. G. Dun and Co. Building, surrounded by smoke in the background. The mass of onlookers are facing Sacramento Street with the Kohl Building on the far left, thought to be fireproof. Two sequence photographs taken on Montgomery from California Street looking north. — Edith Irvine photographs; James Irvine Collection

Refugees with their meager belongings heading uphill to escape the advancing flames.
Taken from an unidentified location. — Edith Irvine photograph; James Irvine Collection

Telegraph Hill in the wake of the fire.
Keystone View Co. - Stereo

for which I am very thankful as I will have a place to work. I am going to guard the store tonight.

The soldiers have shot several thieves, yet I dare say, there is any amount of robbery going on. The city hall is a perfect wreck, and they released all the prisoners yesterday morning; there were 400.

Have just been to look at the fire again. It is a regular Hell on earth. I do not know whether they can stop it or not. The breeze is fanning it, and it is traveling like wild.

We are at this time very uncertain as to how long we will be able to stay in our home,

Top: Smoke and ash swirl above a residential area.
Bottom: Refugees with belongings at the bottom of Russian Hill.
Top: Taken from an unknown location. Bottom: Taken from Fort Mason looking south. — Edith Irvine photographs; James Irvine Collection

Top: Dense plumes of smoke form a frightful backdrop to the scene of a largely residential neighborhood.
Bottom: Soldiers bivouacked at a small courtyard. The second man from left cradles a small dog.
Both taken from unidentified locations. — Gina Janelli Collection

Top: Debris of damaged chimneys atop roofs in the foreground frame the ominous smoke in the background.
Bottom: A dead horse lies among the rubble in the Produce Area, while an armed soldier stands guard.
Top: Taken from Nob Hill looking south. Bottom: Taken from Davis, up Commercial Street. — Edith Irvine photographs; James Irvine Collection

Top: The shaken Girls' High School at Geary and Scott streets.
Bottom: Settled houses, built over made-land in the Mission District.
Top: Taken from Geary looking northeast. Bottom: Taken on Howard Street above 17th Street looking east. — Darrell Colwell Collection

as the fire is burning at 17th & Howard and 14th & Valencia.

Elsie will probably be burned out in about two hours unless they are able to check the fire. They are blowing up buildings in the path of the fire, and in that way they are able to control it, sometimes.

We are packing up our things and will be ready to leave as soon as necessary. Our home was not damaged, and our water has been running all the time. We are living in a tent on the hill as are hundreds of families who were burned out.

When I left home at 6 o'clock this

Ham-and-Eggs Fire

The Fire was the result of a multitude of fires, some of which were given names. One of these was the Hayes Valley Fire, better known by the nickname that reflected something of its cause. The sobriquet, Ham-and-Eggs Fire, almost humanizes what was in reality an especially terrible calamity.

This inferno started at 95 Hayes Street, just east of Gough, when a woman cooked breakfast, apparently unaware that the chimney flue in her two story frame house had been damaged by the temblor. Sparks from the stove set the wall afire. With fire companies tied up elsewhere, this breakfast carelessness was off to a quick start. There is little wonder then that Ham-and-Eggs grew to wipe out an area greater than any other single fire that started with The Earthquake. St. Ignatius Church and College stood on Hayes Street at Van Ness. This was the finest building belonging to the Jesuit Order anywhere on the planet. One is left to wonder why the Jesuits had failed to take out fire insurance on their building, soon to be a total loss.

The Mechanics Pavilion and the St. Nicholas Hotel lay in the path of destruction. When the fire jumped Larkin Street, the severely damaged City Hall burned, consuming most of the government records. Fire Department heroics checked the conflagration at Octavia Street and Golden Gate Avenue. Eventually, the Ham-and-Eggs Fire partnered with flames moving from South of the Slot, thus beginning a fast moving assault on the Mission District, a tide of heat and smoke that would reach to and sweep past the ill-fated Valencia Hotel.

The Ham-and-Eggs Fire viewed from the Western Addition District, looking across McAllister Street. The twin towers of St. Ignatius Church and College loom up to the right. City Hall can be seen left of center in the background.
Taken down Fulton Street looking southeast. — Gina Janelli Collection

evening, the fire had not reached us yet but was very near. The College of Notre Dame, which is just across from Mission Dolores, was one mass of flames when I left. We have all our things on the hill where they will be safe.

Friday, Day 3 (20th)

It is now 2:15 a.m. and I have just finished making my rounds. I am armed with a .38 caliber Colt revolver and my face and hands are black. There are some pretty tough looking characters prowling around down here, and we are watching them close as I do not think they would hesitate a moment about breaking into the store.

There are people camping just across from the store in the railroad yards, and their condition is serious. They have no food and are getting desperate. They look at you with angry looks, and I really think that the only thing which keeps them from attacking us is the fact that we are fully armed.

Roasted bodies are numerous in this locality. They are in most cases on the sidewalks and are mostly men who were probably drunk and could not get away. It was cold and foggy, and the poor people who are sleeping out suffered considerably.

Have just taken another walk and a fireman told me that the fire had been stopped at 20th St., so Elsie I guess is safe. He did not know how far up the valley the fire had burnt, so I did not know whether our home was burnt or not.

Geology and Geography

The fortunes of San Francisco have revolved around major natural factors, perhaps more so than for any other modern great city. For instance, San Francisco Bay offers the most ideal port setting in the world. The counterpoint to such good fortune lies in The City's proximity to the San Andreas Fault, a 750 mile long demarcation between two great tectonic plates, slabs of crustal earth in turmoil, positioned and repositioned through time by gyrating undercurrents emanating from the earth's constantly agitated mantle and below that a vortex of molten heavy metal, the earth's core.

Some plates pull away from one another. Other plates confront each other, and when they do we mortals might be treated rudely. Confrontation sometimes involves one plate subducting under another, or could involve head-on collision or could involve one plate moving with extreme malice against its neighboring antagonist, exactly the case in 1906 when the Pacific Plate struck-slipped past the North American Plate. Most earthquakes, incidentally, happen at the margins of plates.

Varied offsets then occurred along 270 miles of the San Andreas Fault between Hollister and Cape Mendocino. The greatest offset, 21 feet, happened at Olema, between Tomales and Bolinas bays, and nearly due east of Point Reyes. This location is a little further than 25 miles from San Francisco in a northwest direction.

The epicenter is placed elsewhere, under the ocean, one mile offshore, and near Daly City. Point of information - the point from which an earthquake's shock waves radiate (the point of origin) is called the focus; the epicentrum, or epicenter, however, is the point directly above the focus on the surface of the lithosphere. The San Andreas fault line runs more or less straight between the epicenter to the place of maximum surface displacement, Olema, and seaward off the Golden Gate.

The Mutual Life Insurance Building; people on California Street watching the fire, in photos #1 & #2, soon fled. The cabinet and file drawers in the foreground of photo #2 were placed there to protect their contents from the advancing inferno.
All is destruction in Photo #3.

The Mutual Life Insurance Building

Inside the Mutual Life Insurance Building at the center was a feed company, the San Francisco and North Pacific Railroad Company, the Canadian Bank of Commerce, and Mutual Life Insurance. The building to the left housed Wenderath and Turner, Printers. The Fireman's Fund Insurance Company is at the right on California Street.

Three sequence photographs, taken from California and Sansome streets looking southeast.

Edith Irvine photographs; James Irvine Collection

The Hall of Justice as seen from Portsmouth Square before it burned.
Taken from Portsmouth looking west. — Edith Irvine photograph; James Irvine Collection

St. Dominic's at Bush and Steiner streets. The sign at the lower right identifies the temporary location of the Pacific States Telephone and Telegraph Company. The company had been burned out at Bush Street, between Grant and Kearney.

Taken from Stenier Street between Bush and Sutter looking north. — Gina Janelli Collection

At center background is the fire ravaged Palace Hotel.
Taken down Montgomery toward Market Street looking south. — Edith Irvine photograph; James Irvine Collection

The Major Hostelries

The most celebrated of San Francisco's hotels were the Palace, the Grand, the St. Francis, and the Fairmont. The first two hostelries were in the area then called South-of-the-Slot.

The Palace, which opened in 1875, was the largest, and at the time was generally regarded as the world's finest hotel. Few who stayed there would ever forget its covered court or the bay windows overlooking Montgomery and Market streets.

Among the Palace's guests when the temblor occurred was Enrico Caruso who had performed at the Grand Opera House on the night of the seventeenth. A perhaps somewhat apocryphal account has the tenor fleeing the hotel completely terrified. In his nightshirt, he shouted out, "Give me Vesuvius," which seems a bit too contrived and dramatic for a man supposedly scared out of his wits. He later added something about The City being a Hell of a place and vowed never to return. He never did.

By late afternoon on the 18th, the Palace was starting to burn, but employees fought gallantly with anything at hand, including the hotel's own hydrant system, to quell the growing inferno. When a fire company tapped into this water supply to fight a nearby blaze, the fate of the Palace was sealed. The hotel was burned out by early evening. After the Fire, it was demolished, its 30 million bricks carted away to make room for a new Palace, which was rebuilt in 1909.

Next to go, and standing but a short distance northeast of the Palace at the corner of Annie Street and Market, there was the older Grand Hotel. It had signed in its first guests in 1870.

Unlike the Palace and the Grand which were situated at an interface of the Financial District and South of Market District, the St. Francis was just across the street from Union Square on Powell Street, close to the Theater District. A new wing was being added at the time of The Earthquake. Gutted by The Fire, the first two wings were refurbished and the third wing was eventually completed. In the interim, a temporary St. Francis was constructed directly in Union Square.

Interestingly, it was to the St. Francis that the great Caruso had retreated for breakfast, and calmly enough the tenor added to his greatness by consuming a hearty meal. He spent that night a refugee, well pampered no doubt, either at the Presidio or Golden Gate Park, and the next day his entourage proceeded to Oakland, where the Metropolitan Opera Company boarded a train and departed the Bay Area.

The massive Fairmont Hotel stood majestically atop Nob Hill beyond Chinatown at California and Mason. It had been built on property purchased by Senator James Fair, or "Slippery Jim," one of the all Irish "Nevada Four" who had made vast fortunes in the Comstock. When this "Silver King," or "Bonanza King," died before he could erect a mansion on the site, his daughters chose to construct the hotel. It stands next to the house built for another "Silver King," James C. Flood. "Slippery Jim" had wanted a home as opulent as that of Mark Hopkins, one of the "Railroad Kings" or "Big Four" of the Central Pacific.

Constructed on the model of Greek Revival style, the Fairmont was close to being completed. Only on the 19th did the Fairmont catch fire. Its white marble walls turned dark, although their structural integrity remained. The interior, however, fared poorly and had to be done over, including changing out of most of the interior steel framing.

Nearby the Mission, tents went up in Dolores Park.
Taken within the park, between 18th and 20ths streets. — Mission Dolores Collection

Martial Law

San Francisco's citizenry took as gospel that an official declaration of martial law had occurred. The rumor of martial law did not start as a peoples' rumor. After all, Mayor Schmitz had declared, illegally as it turned out, that looters would be shot.

The *Call-Chronicle-Examiner* publication of April 19 carried false and conflicting reports that a declaration of martial law had been issued by President Roosevelt himself, but also laid martial law to a declaration by Schmitz and his Chief of Police. Later the *Examiner* wrongly identified General Funston as the source of such a declaration. The governor did order the state militia onto the streets of The City, but this could be done legally without a proclamation of a state of insurrection, the prerequisite for any legal declaration of martial law.

Later we made a determined effort at these points and thanks to the wideness of Dolores Street and the new Park — two blocks square between 18 & 20 and Dolores & Church — we were able to stop it at these points.

The most critical stage of the fight was when the Notre Dame Convent was burning. It is a very large four story frame building and as it blazed furiously, people held their breaths. The fate of Eureka Valley hung in the balance.

The firemen had two streams of water which they kept playing on the front of the building. As it burned away, the whole front fell back over the fire and partially smothered it. People fell down on their knees and

A *"ghost picture" created from an earlier photograph of the Notre Dame Convent,*
and below a photograph of the collapsed shell of the building after the fire.
Both taken from 16th Street looking southeast down Dolores Street, across from the Mission. — Mission Dolores Collection

Perhaps Edith Irvine's most dramatic photograph of The Earthquake and Fire. Horses lie dead in an alley from collapsed walls in the Produce District. Taken from Davis Street, up Clay. — Edith Irvine photograph; James Irvine Collection

thanked God for this act of providence which saved hundreds of homes.

No sooner was the danger averted at this point than another arose just as serious at 19th & Dolores. The fire was traveling at a great rate at this point, and in order to stop it, it was necessary to blow up the entire square block between 19th & 20th.

◆

Dynamiting on Van Ness Avenue helped to save part of The City. As the fire roared up from Chinatown on the second day, it consumed Nob Hill as it headed west. Army officers realized they had to create a major firebreak or lose the rest of The City to flames. The opportunity came in the upscale area of Van Ness Avenue. Mansion after mansion, including the home of Claus Spreckels, lined the 125-foot-wide causeway. The soldiers went from door to door, ensuring that all occupants of the area were moved out, before dynamiting entire blocks along the east side of the avenue. The firefighters were able to halt the wall of flame with the exception of California Street, where the blaze jumped the street between Clay and Bush, taking out the four-block area. All that was now threatened stood north and east of Russian Hill.

By late Friday evening, only the city wharves and piers were in jeopardy. Fireboats were brought around to North Beach to fight the fire, and a few fire wagons were pulled into the area. With the last of the fires put out, much of The City lay ravaged, and more than half of its citizens were homeless.

Crumbled by earthquake, scourged by fire, and demolished by dynamite, four square miles of San Francisco lay open to the sky. It had been the most horrific catastrophe of peacetime twentieth-century America.

◆

Explosives

In the misguided belief that explosives offered an effective firefighting tool, black powder (saltpeter, sulfur and charcoal), gun cotton (cellulose nitrate), and dynamite (then containing nitroglycerin) were all put to service, but mostly by persons not trained in demolitions.

The aphorism that ignorance is bliss was stood upon its head with witness to counterproductive efforts that blasted fire in myriad directions, split water pipes, and razed structures that might otherwise have served as fire walls. With complete justification, San Francisco's great calamity might have been called "The Earthquake, Fire and Explosive Demolition."

In the aftermath of the tragedy, with booster sentiment denying the full role of a seismic component, obviously any reference to human folly was avoided.

A lone burnt tree stands as a symbol for the greater destruction beyond.
Taken from Nob Hill looking southwest. — Edith Irvine photograph; James Irvine Collection

Special Section
Panoramas of The Fire

"The fire is nearly all out now and we can breathe easy. You cannot imagine the strain it is on a person to be in this uncertain frame of mind never knowing at what minute you will be compelled to jump and run. This whole thing seems like a dream." — Al Cook

Photographers overflowed San Francisco during and after The Earthquake and Fire, and tens of thousands of images were made of nearly every conceivable event and circumstance. A few of those professionals were prepared to do the extraordinary — to photograph in panorama.

A. Blumberg, A. C. Pillsbury, G. R. Lawrence, and F. E. Strohmeier were four men who took hundreds of photographs, many in panorama. All professionals, they made many photographs during and after The Fire, selling them even years later.

Blumberg employed a traditional camera using glass plates. His wide images of The Fire however, have panoramic qualities. His photograph published here shows the Financial District in flames.

Pillsbury, in contrast, took sweeping photographs from a specially constructed camera. This allowed a roll of film, up to five feet in length, to pass in front of the lens as the camera panned the scene. Here, his photography offers a spectacular interplay of light and dark as backdrop to a doomed city.

Lawrence developed the "Captive Airship," a series of kites strung together to loft his 45-pound camera to heights of up to 1,500 feet. He returned three years later to take the panoramic scene from the same position. Lawrence's art captures an eerie desolation.

Strohmeier's technique was to photograph in sections and assemble them in the darkroom later on. His panoramas therefore show seams; however, they are quite long. One of Strohmeier's panoramas is unusual since he panned west to north.

Panorama photography allowed views unattainable with a standard photograph, and it provided the best means to show the extent of the destruction of The Fire.

Two Blumberg panoramas taken from the Fairmont Hotel, April 18th, looking southeast.

From The Story of the Great Disaster

A. C. Pillsbury panorama taken from the St. Francis Hotel, April 18th, looking southeast.
A. C. Pillsbury Collection

G. R. Lawrence panoramas, taken from over Nob Hill looking southeast in May 1906 and April 1909.

Ray Co.

Copyright by F.E. Strohmeier

F. E. Strohmeier panorama taken from the Post Office rooftop after The Fire, looking north. Hibernia Bank at front center, lower photo, on the northwest corner of McAllister Street and Jones Street. These photographs are one panoroma shot.

From The Story of the Great Disaster

Before noon on April 19, horrified onlookers at the west side of Valencia Street watched the advancing Ham-and-Eggs Fire. They were not far from the Valencia Hotel where rescuers were working frantically to free those trapped in the collapsed boarding house. The sign over the doorway of the shop at the right reads "Asahi & Co." Below that, the two words, "Japanese Art."

Taken from Sycamore and Valencia streets looking west. — Edith Irvine photograph; James Irvine Collection

Chapter 3
Into The Burned Area

"The stench down near the store is getting very bad owing to the dead horses and even human beings which are still lying around. The soldiers are going to burn them today, and it will be a good thing." — Al Cook

Saturday came with a stillness that had not been possible in decades. There was no city, and there was no fire. Standing at the corner of Market Street and Van Ness Avenue one witnessed vast devastation to the northeast. This was the Burned Area, and it was being guarded from unauthorized entry.

"You absolutely cannot enter the burned area without a pass," went the refrain. Passes had to be dated, signed and verified, but unless a legitimate need was presented, a pass was not issued. Southwest of the Burned Area, much of the Mission District had also burned. The fire had been stopped at Dolores Street largely because of dynamiting. Below Dolores, the Valencia Hotel, which had collapsed into the ground, had been finished off by flames.

The namesake of Mission Dolores had contributed significantly to the collapse of the Valencia Hotel and to the unsettling of other wood-frame buildings in the neighborhood. The reference here is to the Laguna de los Dolores, a lake long hidden beneath the landscape by fill. With the quake, liquefaction occurred within this area of "made-ground."

Valencia, Howard, Shotwell, and Harrison, plus 11th, 14th, 17th, and 20th streets, all in the Mission District, subsided, causing gaping craters. All but two of the collapsed streets in San Francisco were here. The rapid falling of Valencia and Harrison streets crushed two of the three primary water arteries coming into The City.

South of the Slot, and three miles away, the office and warehouses of the Pacific Hardware and Steel Company were shaken, but were miraculously untouched by the fire. Al obtained passes to go into the burned area each day, walking downhill to go to work and uphill to return home.

Made-Ground

"Made-ground" refers to fill material added on to property. In San Francisco, where fill had been dumped atop once swampy areas or where fill was deposited to extend bayside land, the ground, if shaken violently, was particularly vulnerable to liquification. In fancy terms, made-ground is thixotropic. Buildings constructed over such unstable "made-ground" were at risk of sinking into the surface and collapsing.

The Valencia Street Hotel had sat atop such an unstable environment, as had City Hall, and land at the northeastern end of Market Street, near water's edge, was especially thixotropic.

The destroyed Charles Crocker home. Along with Collis Huntington, Mark Hopkins, and Leland Stanford, Crocker was one of the "Big Four" who built the Central Pacific Railroad, the western segment of the transcontinental railway.

Taken from California Street at Taylor looking north.
Darrel Colwell Collection

John Alphonso Cook
Saturday, Day 4 (21st)
Mission District, San Francisco

I don't know if this is the 21st or not. It seems ages since this reign of terror of the 20th century began. Went down to the store again, but was sent home to get some sleep. I feel better as we had a good feed consisting of eggs, hot buns, rice and tea, and one orange divided between us: Mother, Sister, Dick (Sister's beau), and myself. There is little or no fruit to be had.

I am going to send Mother and Sister to our Aunt's, who is at Elmhurst [in Oakland]. We will pack just what we want to save, and store it in a friend's basement, then leave the house to some poor people. The soldiers are keeping a very strict watch on everybody, and everything.

They caught a man stealing on our block and tied him to the lamp post. He took a match from his pocket and burned through the rope and started to run. He was shot dead in his tracks. There are dozens of people, mostly men, shot every day for stealing, drinking, and disobeying orders. They pick the bodies up and burn them. They are also shooting all the stray dogs which they see around as they are afraid of spreading disease.

Food is not scarce as yet, so there has been no suffering in that respect that I have heard of, although down near the store it is very bad. The people down there are a low class and spend most of their time fighting. They don't seem to know better, and there were several

Top: *Union Street, when traveled east as far as Van Ness, takes one to the western edge of the northern burned area.*
Top: Taken on Union Street looking north. — Edith Irvine photograph; James Irvine Collection
Bottom: *Saint Francis Church of the Assi.*
Bottom: Taken from Vallejo Street looking north. — Darrel Colwell Collection

Refugees

Uncounted numbers of earthquake and fire victims quickly departed San Francisco, some never to dwell there again. Many people found temporary residence with relatives and friends in The City, across the Bay, or down the Peninsula. Many transported tents and other camping equipment in retreat from their burning neighborhoods and sought refuge in parks and vacant lots. There were those who had lost virtually everything and were uncertain how they might secure any shelter. In quick time, however, several housing possibilities materialized, especially for refugees in great need.

Least appealing were the small makeshift hovels cobbled together by individuals using salvage from devastated neighborhoods. These shelters were often constructed away from designated refugee camps having sanitation services, medical aid, food, and clothing distribution.

The Committee for Housing and the Homeless preferred that refugees who remained in San Francisco take up residence at the parks, squares, and other settlement sites overseen by military personnel, where there were such amenities as latrines and communal bathing and laundry facilities. The mounting humanitarian effort engineered by San Francisco's leading citizens was driven in part by the economic necessity to pool together and keep safe a body of workers for the restoration of The City.

Military authorities hurriedly made tents available for a time until the soldiers reclaimed them for their own use. Barracks that divided into small apartments were built. So were "earthquake cottages," those two- and three-room dwellings whose occupancy required a small rent of two dollars a month. There was the option of applying

(continued on next page)

shot yesterday. They don't bother about arresting people now, they just shoot.

The stench down near the store is getting very bad owing to the dead horses and even human beings which are still lying around. The soldiers are going to burn them today, and it will be a good thing.

All fires must be out at 8 o'clock, and after that if you have one you are very apt to be shot. An old lady was shot last night for having a light in her house which she refused to put out.

Have not seen Golda or Elsie, but their homes were not burned so I guess they are all right. There are the tents and other shelters the people have erected all around us. One can hardly believe that so many people who a few days ago owned lovely homes and clothes & etc. are reduced to one suit — all that they can call their own. It is about 8 o'clock now so must begin to work as there is lots to do.

Another day has passed, and I have just returned from a hard days work down at the store, tired but happy in the thought that I still have a home to go to, which is something that thousands cannot do in this city at the present time. I can hardly see to write, for darkness is fast creeping on, and we are not allowed to have a light of any description, but I will try a little longer.

Douglas was over to see me yesterday, but I was not home. He was not burned out, and his folks moved home yesterday. The rooms are also saved for which we are thankful. I called at Elsie's on my way down to work yesterday, but she was not in. Have not heard from Golda, *but I guess she is all right as the fire did not get out her way. Maggie Ryan's home is burned.*

The fire is nearly all out now, and we can breathe easy. You cannot imagine the strain it is on a person to be in this uncertain frame of mind never knowing at what minute you will be compelled to jump and run. This is all I can see to write now so will finish in the morning.

Sunday, Day 5 (22nd)

It is now 5:00 a.m. and I am up and dressed. If anyone should have told me that I would ever be writing at 5:00 a.m. in the morning I would have called them crazy, but there are lots of strange things happening now so I guess it's all right. We go to bed at sunset and get up at sunrise.

It is a sight to look down the streets and see the people all cooking, some on camp fires and some of the more fortunate on stoves. This whole thing seems like a dream. The relief trains are coming in fast now, so I don't think there will be much more suffering.

The soldiers are herding all the loafers they can find around and putting them to work cleaning the streets, burying the dead, and doing other useful things. If they refuse to work, they are shot.

The fire burned north of Market clear over to the bay but did not cross Van Ness Avenue except between Hayes & Golden Gate Avenue, where it burned out to Octavia. South of Market, it burned everything to Townsend Street, and out to Dolores and 20th. On Howard Street, it stopped at 16th.

rent towards the purchase price of 50 dollars. If a family opted to have their simple dark green bungalow removed to a rented lot, their money would be refunded.

At the peak of their use, nearly 16,500 housed families. Over 5,300 "earthquake cottages" were moved. Today, there are about 22 left in San Francisco. If one encountered a surviving "earthquake cottage" in The City, it would likely be barely recognizable for the exterior and interior improvements over the past ten decades. Two are preserved at the Presidio.

A number of cable cars became available for habitation when their services were no longer required. The circumstances were electric cars replacing Market Street cables. With their running gear and wheels removed, the temporary homes were set upon foundations and their exteriors dressed up. One much photographed clustering of cable car houses was in the Richmond District at California Street and 5th Avenue.

Refugee camp on Telegraph Hill.
Griffith & Griffith Bros., Publishers – Stereo

Top: Piles of brick cover the ground where a building collapsed. The Call Building can be seen in the distance.
Bottom: A scene of great devastation.
Top: Taken from South of Market looking northeast. Bottom: Taken from Nob Hill looking east. — Edith Irvine photographs; James Irvine Collection

Top: Ash drifts through the air shortly after The Fire has ended, coating the skeletons of buildings.
Bottom: Stairs to nowhere. In the background Temple Emanu-El is to the right. Center is the domed roof of The Call.
Top: Taken from an unknown location. Bottom: Taken from Nob Hill looking south. — Edith Irvine photographs; James Irvine Collection

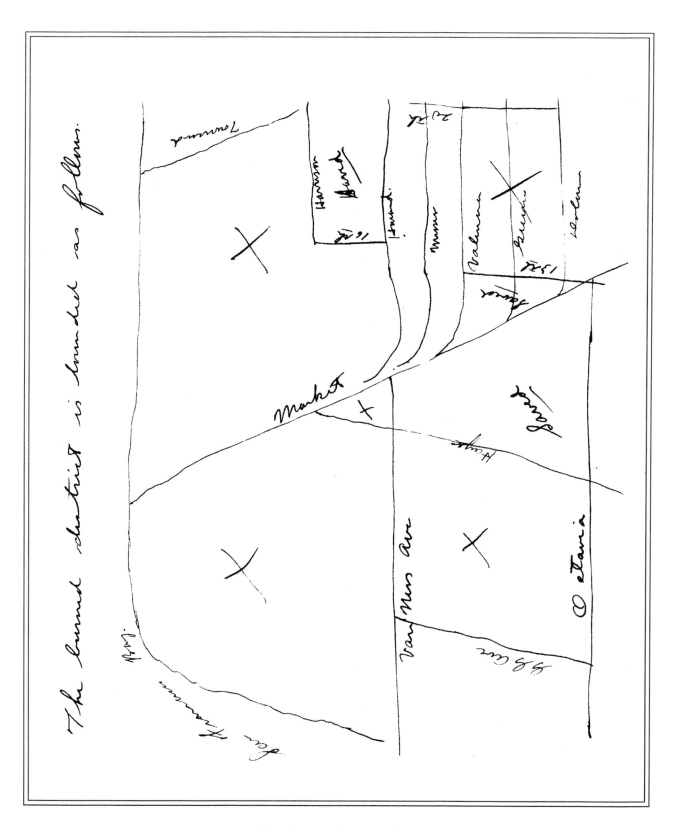

Al Cook's map of the burned area.
Sent with his April 21, 1906 letter. — Private Collection

I am going to try and get a paper today, but you have to fight for them they are so scarce. All the money I have spent since Tuesday is 20 cents. I am going down to the store now. My breakfast was rushed: Hot corn bread, canned apricots, two fried eggs, puffed rice & syrup, and tea. The burned district is bounded as follows. [See map] All the crosses are the burned districts.

Have just finished a frugal meal consisting of pea soup, bread and tea. I have been doing guard duty down at the store all day, and in consequence, I am very tired this evening and my ankle has bothered me a great deal. I must have strained it some way although do not know how.

It has been a blessing to the city to have the store spared because it has enabled the government who have taken charge of the store to supply the people with stoves, pots & pans, & etc. and also the hardware for the temporary homes which they are erecting.

About 3 o'clock, there was another shock, and it was the funniest sight to see the fellows come piling out of the building. They dropped everything and ran helter-skelter, each looking out for themselves. I really think the building will have to be condemned because it creaked and groaned pretty bad yesterday.

They ran the cars on Fillmore Street last night, and they are rushing all work on the street car lines and 'twill not be long before we will have a pretty good car service again. They are going to run electric cars on Market Street as soon as they can blow up the ruins which

Human and Property Toll

The quake began just as the minute hand announced 5:12 AM. At that moment the Pacific Plate lunged suddenly northwest, with the most severe jolt arriving halfway into the first minute of rumbling. With that minute spent, the continuous movement wound down for perhaps another half minute. Quick shocks occurring after that time were within a total duration of approximately two and a half minutes.

Seismic energy of the San Andreas rupture produced a Richter magnitude now estimated at around 7.8. Magnitude is a measure of the size of the ground waves pouring forth from the focus (point of origin). Most of the displacement was horizontal, yet here and there in The City, one witnessed the scars of vertical movements, which, while relatively small in geologic terms, held potential calamity with regard to the well-being of persons and properties.

The greatest number of deaths happened primarily as a result of the shifting earth. It would not be unreasonable to guesstimate that number exceeding 3,000 or more. Ignition of four dozen or so fires followed directly in the immediate aftermath of the shaker. The vast majority of property losses resulted from fire. Scorched acreage is estimated at 2,800, at least ten times that number of buildings were consumed. Up to a quarter of a million persons were left homeless.

When it came time for the skeleton of a city to pick itself up, a myth was actively promoted in recounting the terrible tragedy, one in which, at least indirectly, the image of property trumped that of human life. Specifically, the economic strategy to recover losses through insurance policies and to draw investment monies dictated that an emphasis be placed on The Fire and that The Earthquake be greatly downplayed. Accordingly, city boosters took to calling the tragic event "The Great Fire."

Top: Above the Financial District with electrical wires down on the ground. Felled wires were causes of numerous fires.
Bottom: Two horses at left stand amid the ruins. Horses were often worked to death in the cleanup of the disaster.
Top: Taken from Nob Hill looking southeast. Bottom: Taken from an unknown location. — Edith Irvine photographs; James Irvine Collection

Top: Scene from Montgomery Street of fallen wires and gutted buildings.
Bottom: A scene of devastation, eerily absent of people or animals.
Top: Taken from Montgomery looking toward Market Street. Bottom: An unknown location. — Edith Irvine photographs; James Irvine Collection

A "ghost picture" created from an earlier photograph of the Crocker Mansion and the Stereo below.
Taken from California Street looking northeast. — Private Collection

A photograph of the collapsed shell of the building after the fire with an incenerated automobile in the foreground.
Underwood & Underwood Publishers — Stereo

endanger traffic. They are blowing up ruins now along Market Street, and have gangs of men clearing away the debris.

Monday, Day 6 (23rd)

I stopped writing and went up to see Mabel Drusbach. She is well, and they did not suffer much from the quake. Rob's place of business was burned up, and he is pretty tired from fighting the fire. Their house is full of friends who were burned out. Elsie has gone to Mill Valley. Have not heard from Golda or the other girls yet.

This morning about 2:30 a.m. it began raining, and it came down pretty hard for about an hour. It will make it very hard for those who were living in temporary shelters made out of sheets, because the rain would go right through them. The sun is shining bright and warm this morning so that will enable them to dry their bedding.

I came home from work early today on account of my ankle, which has become quite painful, and has stiffened up so that I can hardly walk.

It rained again a good deal today, and I suppose that a great deal of furniture which had been saved by tireless efforts from the fire was ruined by water. As I went to work this morning, I came across several people who were sitting beside all they had in the world weeping and just about ready to give up. They had been getting along nicely, when up comes this rain and ruins all they had saved. It makes you pretty blue to see all the suffering and not to be able

A shelter built of wreakage near the ruined City Hall.
Taken from Market Street looking north.
Underwood & Underwood Publishers - Stereo

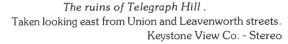

The ruins of Telegraph Hill .
Taken looking east from Union and Leavenworth streets.
Keystone View Co. - Stereo

Top: The Call Building at center. Looking down O'Farrell Street.
Bottom: Tent city at Hamilton Pool Recreation Center on Geary. St. Dominic's at center is on Bush and Steiner.
Top: Taken from O'Farrell looking east. Bottom: Taken from Geary toward Pierce Street looking north. — Darrel Colwell Collection

Top: *Buildings near Union Square.*
Bottom: **The Newman and Levinson Building *(left)* and the Whittell Building *(far right,)* under construction.**
Both taken near Geary Street. — Darrel Colwell Collection

to do anything for them.

Saw Miss Eliz & Miss Lonergan were at the store today. Both families lost everything they had, but are all well and glad they are living. Mother is just coming home from a food hunt and has captured about two dozen soda crackers which are at this time a luxury, a can of mackerel and some other canned stuff. The Lord knows what, but which we are thankful for just the same. The women go out and forage all day for grub, and it's all a gamble what we'll get to eat at night when we come home. It doesn't make much difference what we get now as long as its something to eat.

Emma Spreckels Building on Market Street is in ruins. The sign attached to the beam directs people to the temporary location for one business that had occupied this site. The handwriting on the beam says "Front Beam."
Taken from Turk Street looking east.
Whiting View Co. - Stereo

Two women pose in front of devastated buildings.
Taken from the corner of Ellis and Powell streets, looking northwest. — Stereo View Co. - Stereo

Many people who stayed in The City had lost nearly everything — their jobs, their homes, their furnishings, their clothing, their cooking utensils. Most of what they saved or salvaged, they carried to one of the tent cities stationed throughout The City. So much had been lost by fire, if not the initial earthquake; then it rained.

Saved food stuffs, clothing, and other items were now soaked or ruined. Some items — a victrola or a music box — were saved only to be damaged by the rain. Even a piano was rolled out into Dolores Park, and was then saturated by the downpour.

The ferries continued to operate, and the railroads began to bring in food, clothing, and medical supplies. The local transportation systems came back slowly. The cable cars were put out of service entirely. Many cars were frozen

Top: On Stockton Street looking towards Pine Street, a clear view of the imposing Mills Building on Montgomery Street.
Bottom: The Jackson Brewing Co.
Top: Taken down Montgomery Street toward Market. Bottom: Taken from 11th and Folsom— Edith Irvine photographs; James Irvine Collection

Top: Gutted Flood Building, at the corner of Powell and Ellis streets near Market, in the heart of the Financial District.
Bottom: Mills Building at northeast corner of Bush and Montgomery (left) with the First National Bank at right.
Top: Taken looking southeast; Bottom: Taken from Market Street, just up from Sutter.— Darrel Colwell Collection

Top: Temple Emanu-El on the skyline behind a burned building.
Bottom: Market Street with Hearst Building is at the center and the Call Building at right.
Top: Taken from Union Square looking northwest. Bottom: Taken from O'Farrell Street looking east. — Darrel Colwell Collection

The shell of the Sahlein Building apartments on the northeast corner of Polk and Bush streets.
Taken from Polk and Bush looking northeast. — Gina Janelli Collection

Top: The shell of a dynamited building that once housed the Middleton Motor Car Company on Van Ness.
Taken from Van Ness and Golden Gate Avenue looking east.
Gina Janelli Collection

Contorted steel seen through an entry way.
Taken from an unknown location. — Darrel Colwell Collection

Top: The sad remnants of a once lofty building.
Bottom: Hearst Building at the far left. Whittel Building, the "Birdcage," at the far right.
Top: Taken from an unknown location. Bottom: Taken from Union Square looking south. — Gina Janelli Collection

in the streets and were burned over by the fire. Some survived either to be returned to service or to be moved to make temporary homes.

Makeshift wagons were pressed into service, transporting people who stood on low platforms. Some cable cars eventually came back, but only a few at a time, and never to the extent that they had been before. Of the 90 original cable car miles, some 17 miles were returned to working order.

A fourth of San Francisco was gone, and within that area had been the business, finance, and produce districts, plus the city buildings. Yet San Franciscans moved quickly to start the resurrection of The City.

◆

Lumber wagon pressed into temporary service as a "streetcar."
Underwood & Underwood – Stereo

Top: Hall of Justice with its heavily damaged tower. Located on Kearny Street and facing Portsmouth Square.
Underwood and Underwood – Stereo

Bottom: Looters/scavengers near Montgomery Avenue and Vallejo Street.
Stereo View Co. - Stereo

Close up view of the tower of the City Hall. Perhaps the most photographed building of The Earthquake and Fire.
Taken from near City Hall Avenue looking northwest. — Edith Irvine photograph; James Irvine Collection

Special Section
A Walk in the Devastation

"I went to town and took some pictures of the ruins ... it was seven-thirty before I got home. I had to walk up from the ferry, and it's quite a little hike out to my home." — Al Cook

On *Sunday, April 29th, Al Cook* went downtown to take photographs of what he called "the mix-up." It had been less than two decades since George Eastman had introduced the box camera produced for public use. The Brownie camera cost just $1.00 (perhaps $20.00 today) and held six shots per filmstrip. By 1900 there were 100,000 Brownies in American hands.

In taking his photographs, Al joined many amateur and professional photographers who took thousands of pictures of The Earthquake and Fire. People crossed the bay by ferry or came up the peninsula by train just to view and photograph The Great Disaster. Unknowingly, they became a part of the world's first extensively photographed, great natural disaster.

The remaining residents and visitors alike had literally hundreds of choices in the myriad of souvenir photographs, postcards, and stereo views available to buy.

Auto stereoscopes would show a series of stereo views, one every few seconds. Biographs — one cent machines — would flip up to 1500 photo cards in a simulated movie show. Nickelodeons — five cent movie theaters — could seat up to 70 people, and showed 10 and 20 minute reels of the event. San Francisco's Earthquake and Fire was well documented. Motion pictures also recorded The Great Disaster.

The captured images covered every imaginable scene — refugees camped in parks, broken and burned buildings, and people waiting in food lines. The most photographed scene of The Great Disaster was City Hall. Photographs from every angle, of each broken

Up Telegraph Hill in the Wake of the Earhtquake and Fire - San Francisco Disaster of Ap;ril 18, 1906.
Keystone View Co. — Stereo

column and of fallen statues were available in a variety of images and forms. Photographers also favored Nob Hill mansions, tilted buildings on Howard Street, and the Call Newspaper Building. The Valencia Street Hotel was repeatedly photographed before it was incinerated.

◆

Photographing the ruined city.

Standard Scenic — Stereo

A photographer sets up on Grant Avenue (now Dupont); taken from Market Street.
Stereo View Co. — Stereo

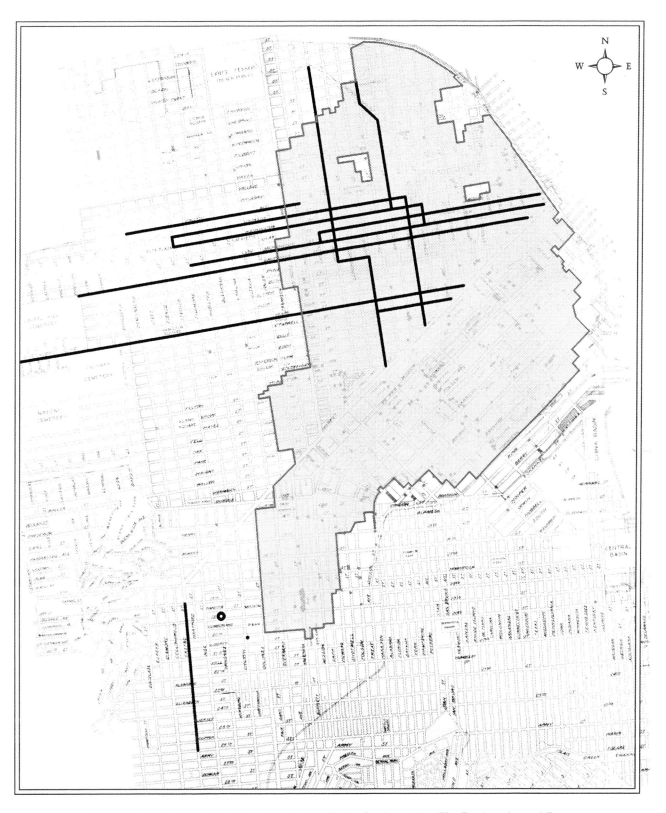

1906 Street Map of San Francisco, showing the Cable Car lines after The Earthquake and Fire.
The Burned Area is shaded, and the dot near Al Cook's Home is a fire hydrant.
Composite Map, Private Collection

Valencia & Howard streets

Both Valencia and Howards streets had Earthquake and Fire damage. Both suffered from the fact that they lay over the lake bed of *Laguna de los Dolores.* Valencia and Harrison streets held two of the water main lines — both crushed during the earthquake. Howard (now South Van Ness) burned only on the west side of the street, but many buildings on the east side sank as did the street itself.

Damaged cable car tracks border two sides of a hole that has opened up. The burned area on the left is the site of the Valencia Street Hotel. The burned area to the right allows an unobstructed view to the dome of City Hall in the distance.
Taken from 19th Street, looking north on Valencia Street. — Gina Janelli Collection

The same hole but looking south. New water pipes have been delivered to both sides of the street for repairs.
Taken from Valencia Street between 18th and 19th looking south. — Gina Janelli Collection

Because of liquifaction, Valencia Street dropped four feet. In some locations, photographers would take nearly the same shot.
Taken from Valencia Street looking south.
H.C. White Co. - Stereo

Buildings on the east side of Howard Street. Furniture and other belongings sit on the sidewalk outside of an apartment building before The Fire. The two settled houses at left were among the most photographed structures of The Earthquake and Fire.
Taken from Howard Street between 16th and 17th looking east. — Gina Janelli Collection

Buildings on the east side of Howard Street after fire reached the neighborhood. The settled houses were built over made-land in the Mission District.
Taken from the burned out side of Howard Street.
H. C. White Co. - Stereo

Top: Buildings on the east side of Howard Street. Note the furniture missing because of the fire across the street.
Taken from Howard Street, between 16th and 17th looking east. — Darrel Colwell Collection
Bottom: Damaged cable car tracks border a hole. Spire of Trinity Lutheran Church on right.
Taken on Howard between 16th & 17th south toward Bernal Heights. — Gina Janelli Collection

City Hall

An integrated imagery of the physical glory and physical ruin of City Hall strikes the perfect metaphor to characterize a political climate in which the Gilded Age was retreating before the Progressive Era. The glitter of City Hall masked poor planning, questionable design, shoddy materials, and substandard workmanship, but more to the point, it gave a mask to the culture of graft and corruption that had festered in San Francisco government. The specter of a once glorious monument stripped of its gilt helped precipitate steps leading first literally and then figuratively to cleaning up City Hall. There was a political firestorm that followed The Fire, bringing added trauma to an already traumatized city.

Tumbled columns at the backside of City Hall.
Taken from Larkin Street looking north. — Edith Irvine photograph; James Irvine Collection

94

Top: City Hall from near Market Street.
Bottom: City Hall from near City Hall Avenue. Photograph used on the cover of this book.
Top: Taken from near Market Street looking east. Bottom: Taken from near City Hall Avenue looking east.
Edith Irvine photographs; James Irvine Collection

*Close-up of City Hall showing the
internal steel construction.*
Taken from near City Hall Avenue looking north.
Edith Irvine photograph; James Irvine Collection

*Similar close-up of City Hall. The City Hall was perhaps
the most photographed ruin of The Earthquake & Fire.*
Taken from near City Hall Avenue looking north.
Darrel Colwell Collection

City Hall from McAllister Street.
Taken from McAllister Street looking south down Larkin.
Edith Irvine photograph; James Irvine Collection

Men standing in the rubble of City Hall.
Taken from Larkin Street looking south.
Edith Irvine photograph; James Irvine Collection

Nob Hill

Crowned with opulent mansions, traveled over by richly appointed carriages, and otherwise reflecting the culture of conspicuous consumption, Nob Hill reflected the Gilded Age tastes of the financial empire in residence. The Hearst newspapers characteristically denounced the "robber barons" living on the Hill, and one can only imagine the spiritual lifting of populist sentiment in this class conscious society when the grandest Nob Hill monuments, built by Mark Hopkins, Leland Stanford, Colis Huntington, Charles Crocker, James Flood and others were turned into ruins in The Great Earthquake and Fire.

Soldiers guarding the Charles Crocker home located on California Street between Taylor and Jones streets.
Taken from California Street at Taylor looking north. — Edith Irvine photograph; James Irvine Collection

Front yard of Crocker home on California Street between Jones and Taylor streets. Portico of the Towne Mansion is at the far right. This portico was removed and later set up in Golden Gate Park at Lloyd Lake.

Taken from California Street looking south.
Darrel Colwell Collection

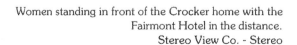

Women standing in front of the Crocker home with the
Fairmont Hotel in the distance.
Stereo View Co. - Stereo

Both photographs are of the Flood Mansion at California and Mason streets on Nob Hill.
James Flood made his first million in the Comstock Lode silver mining industry.
Top: Taken from California Street at Mason looking north. Bottom: Looking west. — Edith Irvine photographs; James Irvine Collection

Top: *Remains of the Hopkins Mansion. Mark Hopkins was one of the "Big Four" railroad barons.*
Taken from California Street at Mason looking east. — Ray Co.
Bottom: Claus Spreckels' residence on Van Ness Avenue, on the outskirts of Nob Hill.
Taken from the corner of Van Ness Avenue and Clay Street looking east. — Edith Irvine photograph; James Irvine Collection

Chinatown

In 1906, Chinatown extended from Sacramento Street to Pacific, and from Portsmouth Square to nearly Powell. An attempt to stop the fire in the Banking District was made using gunpowder. As a consequence a drugstore at the east end of Chinatown was blown up. The resulting fire consumed Chinatown and then roared upward toward the Nob Hill residences.

Looking toward the devastation up Nob Hill. The Fairmont Hotel can be seen in the distance.
Taken near Bush and Stockton streets looking northwest.
Edith Irvine photograph; James Irvine Collection

Looking northeast across Chinatown at Telegraph Hill. Hall of Justice is at the extreme right.
Taken from California Street and Stockton looking northeast.
Edith Irvine photograph; James Irvine Collection

Chinatown as seen from Portsmouth Square.
The Fairmont Hotel is on the Nob Hill skyline.
Taken from Portsmouth Square looking west.
Standard Scene Co. – Stereo

Chinatown

The Chinese in San Francisco comprised a reluctantly tolerated to despised caste, and accordingly, except for house servants to the affluent, the "Celestials" were most concentrated within a rectangular area whose border ran more or less on Broadway between Kearny to Stockton, south on Stockton to California Street, then east to Kearny, and north back to Broadway. Within this rectangle, bisected north-south by Grant Avenue [formerly Dupont], were all manner of sights, sounds, and smells unfamiliar to outsiders at the turn of the century. This greatest single gathering of Chinese in the Western Hemisphere presented an especially odd demo-graphic. It was top heavy with bachelors, the majority of whom had few prospects of siring progeny, a circumstance largely determined by the Chinese Exclusion Act of 1882.

Many businessmen and politicians, lacking the patience to let declining population numbers run their course, agitated for clearing Chinatown of Chinese, leveling their property, and redeveloping the area for white commerce. Indeed, many in the white community thought that their opportunity had arrived when Chinatown was consumed in The Earthquake and Fire.

One measure of the contemporary racial climate is documented in news accounts of events that transpired after Chinatown was vacated and its denizens sent to segregated refugee camps in The City and across the Bay. Chinatown, unlike the rest of San Francisco, was not spared large-scale looting. By most estimates well over a thousand middle-class and society people, male and female, descended upon the razed area, many believing they might find gold, others content just to carry off souvenir plates, cups and saucers, particularly if the chinaware glazes had remelted. Too often

the soldiers surveyed scenes of lawbreakers with detachment, or when indifference gave way, they might themselves appropriate property.

In the course of the authors' research and writing, a wonderful serendipity struck. One of us (DW) was arranging notes for this book on the Amtrak to Santa Barbara from Orange County and aroused the curiosity of a passenger seated nearby, Mrs. Pat Williams. When appraised of the project, she volunteered that she possessed a sugar bowl and creamer that had been scavenged from the gutted Chinese district in 1906. Although the two artifacts had been family heirlooms, she wanted to give them to the senior author. Her largess arrived by mail, and sure enough, each piece of Chinaware displayed tell-tale bubbling, particularly over the outer surfaces. With Pat's enthusiastic support, the two artifacts are now repatriated to the Chinese Historical Society of America and are presently displayed in their museum on Clay Street.

Chinatown in ruins.
Taken from **Washington Street** looking south down **Stockton**.
Stereo View Co. - Stereo

Looking across burned-out Chinatown. The almost finished Fairmont Hotel, crowning Nob Hill, is on Mason Street between Sacramento and California streets, to the upper right. To the side stand stone walls of the James Flood Mansion, its roof missing.

Taken from Keystone View Co. - Stereo

Surveying the damage below the "millionaires district" of Nob Hill. The Fairmont Hotel is in the background.

Taken from Stockton Street looking northwest.
Stereo View Co. - Stereo

Sugar bowl and creamer looted in 1906 and returned to Chinatown in 2006.
Paragon Agency Photo

Houses of Worship

Few churches, synagogues, or temples were left unharmed by The Disaster. Of the best known houses of worship, only Mission Dolores — the source of San Francisco's name — escaped unscathed. The photographs here, depict major religious structures that suffered from the temblor and or fire.

Temple Emanu-El in ruins. One block north of Union Square.
Taken from the corner of Stockton and Sutter streets looking northwest. — Darrel Colwell Collection

Saint Francis Church off of Vallejo Street between Grant Avenue and Montgomery Street.
The Middle of three plaques above the steps reads, "To Almighty God, under the invocation of Saint Francis of Assisium."
Taken from Vallejo Street looking north. — Darrel Colwell Collection

Grace Church after the fire.
Stereo View Co. - Stereo

Old Saint Mary's Church on California Street.
Taken from Nob Hill, looking east toward the Bay.
L. C. Smith – Stereo

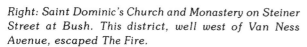

Top: *Earthquake and Fire damaged Congregation Beth Israel Synagogue and the Masonic Scottish Rite Temple. Taken from Geary near Filmore looking south.*

Right: *Saint Dominic's Church and Monastery on Steiner Street at Bush. This district, well west of Van Ness Avenue, escaped The Fire.*
Taken from Steiner near Pine, looking south.
Both Gina Janelli Collection

Houses of Worship

With few exceptions, San Francisco's most recognized houses of worship were not spared trauma from Nature's unleashed energies. Most sustained significant earthquake and/or fire damage. The lone exception was the venerable Mission San Francisco de Asís, opened 130 years before the Earthquake and Fire. It is better known as "Mission Dolores," the nickname derived from the now long disappeared Lake Dolores and Dolores Creek.

The Mission's thick walls had been constructed using mud adobe bricks, and ceiling beams had been lashed together with rawhide. Yet it refused to be moved, but some of the headstones in the cemetery did fracture and fall to the ground or land up against the south wall of the Mission. However, the adjacent Mission Dolores Church was hit hard, but being on the west side of Dolores Street, it remained safe from the flames.

The grandest Jesuit Building in the world stood at Hayes Street and Van Ness Avenue. This was the St. Ignatius Church and College, which succumbed to the Ham-and-Eggs Fire; it was an uninsured loss.

Another well known Catholic structure in this very Catholic city also sustained earthquake but not fire damage. St. Dominic's Church and Monastery, at Steiner near Pine, sits well west of Van Ness Avenue in an area that escaped burning. St. Dominic's became a favorite of '06 photographers.

On California Street, Old St. Mary's and the Episcopal Grace Church showed virtually no outward signs of damage due to the temblor. For a while, it looked as if the Catholic edifice at the corner of Dupont might be spared, as the nearby fire was being contained on a northern boundary at Washington and Battery at the Appraisers Building. Indeed, an enclave of buildings was successfully protected by the heroics of civilians, Marines, and firemen with an Oakland fire engine. However, the eastern front of the fire eventually consumed the interior of Old St. Mary's, but not satisfied, it continued up Nob Hill, successfully stalking Grace Church. The ruins of Grace Church were removed, but the church was not rebuilt at this particular site. Now called Grace Cathedral, its congregation meets elsewhere on Nob Hill, on property donated by the Crocker family.

Old St. Mary's became another favorite of photographers, as all around it had been destroyed, leaving a lone monument of distinctive look. Enough remained of the once beautiful St. Francis Church, off of Vallejo between Grant Avenue and Montgomery Street, to likewise draw many photographers.

Destruction of the Emanu-El Temple on Sutter Street, one block north of Union Square, offers a story that presages the later image of San Francisco as a Mecca for the liberal minded. Almost two decades before The Earthquake and Fire, the local Unitarians were between churches, awaiting the completion of their new building. With no place to worship, Temple Emanu-El graciously offered to share their synagogue. The Unitarians accepted the offer, and the two congregations grew close. When the Temple was burned out in 1906, the Unitarians invited the Jewish congregation to meet at their new church, an arrangement that lasted over a year. Between 1910 and 2004, the two religious groups held joint Thanksgiving Day services. Starting in 2005, the Thanksgiving Service expanded to include more Protestant groups, Catholics, and Muslims in a grand Interfaith get-together.

Refugees settling down at Dolores Park, not far from the Mission. Entailing great effort no doubt, a piano has been transported to the property to keep it out of harm's way. Taken from Church Street and Dolores looking north. — Edith Irvine photograph; James Irvine Collection

Chapter 4
One Week Later

"Old walls and chimneys have been blowing down all day, and it is very dangerous to walk anywhere near them. The wall of the American Company just across the street from us on Townsend blew down and killed a young man who was walking along. It is very fortunate more were not killed." — Al Cook

San Franciscans began to recover from the disaster immediately following The Fire. The many homeless people who remained in The City found housing in makeshift tents and simple shacks constructed from anything available.

Soon, most of these 200,000-plus souls found themselves settled in at parks, empty lots, or the Presidio. Special camps were established throughout The City, with the army, police, and militia coordinating the effort.

The once-independent people of San Francisco now lined up to receive bread, potatoes, fruit, meat, and whatever else was available. Trainloads of donated supplies were arriving from all over America, and donations of money poured in from around the world.

Signs were everywhere, directing people to relocated businesses, informing relatives and friends of the whereabouts of families, advising people not to trespass, and warning of the dangers in burned out and crumbled buildings.

Restaurants, barbershops, and all kinds of service businesses restarted, often in tents or makeshift structures amid the ruins. Other establishments relocated to temporary quarters in buildings that had survived. Various firms moved outside The City, often to Oakland or Berkeley, for up to a year or more. Most however returned to their beloved San Francisco.

All men not found working were gathered together in work details. Removing rubble, collecting bricks, and shoveling ash, they used horse-drawn wagons to cart away the debris. During the next year, thousands of horses died

Start-up restaurant. Unidentified location.
Edith Irvine photograph; James Irvine Collection

Business Resumed

Individual human resourcefulness, economic necessity, and the city fathers' glowing prognostications of commercial growth all played roles, singly or in combination, to motivate people to return to familiar or new employments. Many firms resuming business temporarily across the Bay put up signs to inform customers of new locations. Makeshift barber shops and restaurants sprang up, often adjacent to the ruins of their former business. Professional photographers documented damage for insurance companies and clients who had suffered property loss. Men with special expertise hired out to open cooled down safes. Entrepreneurs transported people in horse drawn wagons along trolley car and street car routes. Horse and buggy drivers offered tours among the ruins. San Francisco was on the mend.

of exhaustion. Of the millions of tons of wreckage, most of it was brought to bayside barges and dumped at the Golden Gate.

Al Cook continued to work at Pacific Hardware and Steel, which for the most part survived The Great Disaster. His duties shifted from guarding the wares to handing them out. With government takeover of certain industries, building materials were given away toward the resurrection of The City.

John Alphonso Cook

Tuesday, Day 7 (24th)

Mission District, San Francisco

One week ago the mix-up began. It seems like a year instead of a week, and the whole affair – earthquake, fire and all – seems like a dream. Yet we have but to go a block or two away, and we can see plenty of evidence which knocks the dream theory on the head.

Wednesday, Day 8 (25th)

I am unable to go to work today on account of my ankle which is worse, and I am going to the hospital to have it attended to. It makes a fellow feel blue to have such a drawback, but I suppose I should be thankful it is not worse.

Today is my sister's birthday, but the poor kid will not have much of a time. We will have to owe her one, until such time as we are able to giver her one. Mother and sister are both well and the out-of-door life seems to agree with both.

There was another shock of earthquake a few moments ago, but it was more rumbling than shake. We are all ready to cut and run every time the house jars. At night I sleep like a log, and never feel the slight shocks which occur nightly, so at least Mother tells me.

Several of the Wai Kai Kai boys are pressed into service and are doing all kinds of work. I saw Bertha's brother Earnest yesterday, drawing a hay wagon, and he

Top: Barber about to resume business at the ruins of his barbershop.
Stereo View Co. - Stereo

Bottom: Bank safes, under guard, in the process of cooling off before opening. The sign says "Safes Watched."
Stereo View Co. - Stereo

Site of Shreve & Company, Jewelers, at northwest corner of Post Street and Dupont (Grant) Avenue.
Taken from Post Street looking northeast. — Darrel Colwell Collection

Shreve & Company, Jewelers

The Shreve & Company Beaux Arts building at Post Street opened for business on March 19, 1906. The steel frame edifice was built to rigorous seismic standards.

Just after the shock, loyal employees secured jewelry, time pieces, and other valuables in a huge safe. The vault and its contents came through in excellent shape, as did the building's frame. However, elegant showcases and other accoutrements fell victim to fire.

A containment was constructed around the vault and infantry soldiers stood guard in the gutted showroom. After three weeks cooling off, the vault was opened.

Business resumed briefly at Post Street, but then the firm took up temporary residence in Oakland before returning to San Francisco in 1909. Visitors to Shreve & Company will see an exterior little changed from 1906, and the showroom's original marble columns are in place.

The 1852 location of the Shreve brothers first jewelry store was nearby, but it did not survive The Fire. An 1852 start-up date for a high-end luxury business is testimony to the sudden wealth conferred upon The City from the Mother Lode Country.

seemed to think it great sport. Have not seen or heard of Golda yet as she has not reported at the store since the quake. I guess the poor girl is afraid to venture among the ruins which surround the store.

Thursday, Day 9 (26th)

Nothing very exciting has happened today, and I spent most of it sitting around reading. Adolph Wagner, one of the boys, came to the house this morning and informed me that there was to be a meeting of the board of directors of the fraternity this afternoon, and as I am a member of that body I was forced to hobble over there.

District Attorney Langdon wanted our rooms for his offices as all the courts or at least most of them are to be held in the building until such time as they can move into the new city hall, and the Lord only knows when that will be as it took them twenty-one years to build the last one. It only took twenty-one seconds to completely destroy the old one, so you can see how rotten it must have been. Let us hope they will put up a much better one next time.

Langdon and his crew of grafters were very much surprised and disconcerted when they found that we did not run or get down on our knees when they came in, intending no doubt to sweep all before them. They were politely but firmly informed that the Wai Kai Kai were a corporation under the laws of the state of California and held a legal lease on the rooms for a term of two years. Also that

Shreve & Company building.
Taken from Dupont looking north. — Courtesy of Shreve & Co.

115

Top: A family has moved their stove to curbside. To prevent fires, citzens were ordered not to cook in their homes.
Bottom: Empty boxes and bags in hand, men and women line up at a food distribution center.

Both taken from unknown locations. — Gina Janelli Collection

*Top: Men, women and children, many consciously posed for a group portrait, stand in front of a refugee camp in an open area.
Bottom: A refugee tent camp in Duboce Park, with Buena Vista Park in the background.*

Top: Taken from an unknown location. Bottom: Taken from Steiner looking north. — Gina Janelli Collection

they could not be compelled to give up their rooms as long as such condition lasted, but were willing to sell the lease at a reasonable figure.

Jim Davis, our attorney, slipped them this parcel of information, and if you never saw a surprised bunch of men in your life you should have seen them. They of course said that they would consider our offer, and if they want the rooms, they'll have to come through with a goodly wad which will not doubt break their hearts but which will put us on a very fine financial standing.

Mr. Hearst and his relief corps took it upon themselves to enter our rooms during the night and appropriate such furniture as they thought they would need, and as such an act is unlawful, Mr. Hearst will be called upon to pay for all he has used. They returned some of those beautiful tables and chairs, and they are ruined. We can buy stamps now so I'll be poor again.

Friday, Day 10 (27th)

This morning about eleven o'clock the wall of the American Company just across the street from us on Townsend, blew down and killed a young man who was walking along. It is very fortunate more were not killed as there has been of late a great many people walking down Townsend St.

I have just come up from our basement where I have been working hard for the last few moments in conjunction with our wood pile. My foot felt fine this morning so I went

Refugee tent city at Golden Gate Park.
Stereo View Co. - Stereo

On Turk Street looking north across a breadline at Jefferson Square, the location of one of many tent cities and a burial ground for unidentified dead.
Stereo View Co. - Stereo

Top: Stairs leading to a tent city in Alamo Square. Personal belongings stacked along the sidewalk.
Taken from corner of Sanchez Street and Grove Street. — Gina Janelli Collection

Bottom: Refugee camp. Tents provided by the military. Unidentified location. — Darrel Colwell Collection

Political Scene

City District Attorney William Langdon and "his crew of grafters" had sought to appropriate for the D. A.'s office rooms leased by Wai Kai Kai, Al Cook's fraternal order. Wai Kai Kai was headquartered in the building at 312A Gurrero Street.

The courts were to be held in this building until a new City Hall could be built. Al Cook offered this commentary" "...Lord only knows when that will be as it took them twenty-one years to build the last one. It took only twenty-one seconds to completely destroy the old one so you can see how rotten it must have been."

Indeed, the earthquake had laid bare the graft that had attended the long ago construction of City Hall. For instance, supporting columns that should have been sturdy were hollow, and brick walls that should have been solid were instead filled with debris.

Al Cook's bias against Langdon was in part rooted in his distaste for the corruption infesting city government. Also, he counted himself a Progressive, but Langdon had won his office on the Schmitz-Ruef slate, backed by San Francisco's Union Labor Party. However, in the political turmoil following The Earthquake and Fire, Langdon at the behest of former Mayor James Phelan and his cohorts investigated Mayor Eugene Schmitz and political boss Abraham Ruef, both of whom were justifiably brought up on charges of bribery and extortion. Langdon had gubernatorial aspirations. In 1907, Schmitz was convicted for taking bribes but spent only a short while in county jail. A successful appeal overturned the conviction. Ruef had no such luck. Convicted, he served a much longer four and a half year term in state prison. It would be interesting to know Al Cook's opinion of Langdon following what was partly an anti-Semitic scapegoating of Ruef.

In the same letter there was brief mention of a dustup in the making between the Wai Kai Kais and William Randolph Hearst's Los Angeles Examiner Relief Corps. (Hearst also owned the San Francisco Examiner.) The Relief Corps, composed mainly of a large group of doctors and nurses, was transported by chartered train from Los Angeles mainly to give medical aid to the stricken city. With a contingent of reporters on board, Hearst must also have had in mind newspaper promotion and self-aggrandizement. (Hearst too had gubernatorial ambitions, but for New York.) Apparently, some members of the group illegally helped themselves to such tables and chairs as they had need of. Some of the furniture came back damaged, and the fraternity would call for Hearst to pay for what the Corps had unlawfully used.

Refugee tent camp in the east end of the Panhandle, at Baker Street. McKinley Monument was erected in 1904. — Gina Janelli Collection

Ramshackle housing and tents on an unidentified lot.

Gina Janelli Collection

Moulder School distribution station. Tons of flour in white sacks. Destroyed City Hall at upper right.
Stereo View Co - Stereo

down to work, and it did not bother me all day for which you can bet your bottom dollar, I was thankful. I guess the tight bandages did the trick as they held the ankle in place.

It has been blowing a gale today, making it almost impossible to walk. The dust and ashes flying around are something fierce. My eyes and ears were full of them when I got home this evening. Old walls and chimneys have been blowing down all day, and it is very dangerous to walk anywhere near them.

Hale Bros. Inc. (missing an "H") is no more; south building.
Taken from Market Street looking southeast. — Edith Irvine photograph; James Irvine Collection

Top: People milling about the destroyed Hale Bros. Inc. after much of the rubble has been carted away.
Bottom: Offering bread and drink in front of Hale Bros. Inc.
Taken from Market Street looking southeast. — Darrel Colwell Collection

Edith Irvine photograph; James Irvine Collection

The wasteland of an unidentified area.

Saturday, Day 11 (28th)

It seems that a day cannot pass without something terrible happening. First it was deaths by earthquake, next by fire, and now by wind. What will be next? It rained and blew like the very old last night but thank goodness most of the people have been cared for so it did not make so much difference. Ma is at the piano waiting for me to come and sing so I go for a little while and then to bed.

Sunday, Day 12 (29th)

I went to town and took some pictures of the ruins and then went across the bay and called on Olive and your Mother, and although I left at about four o'clock, it was seven-thirty before I got home. I had to walk up from the ferry, and it's quite a little hike

William Randolph Hearst brought 25 trains, fully loaded with food and supplies for San Francisco.
Private Collection

Buildings with triangle shaped roof at center of unidentified area.
Edith Irvine photograph; James Irvine Collection

out to my home.

Met Douglas on the boat and he walked out to Golden Gate with me. Your Mother and Olive and Will all look fine and I was glad to see them so. Did not see your Father.

Had quite a long talk with Mr. and Mrs. Johnson, and "they and all that belongs to them are well although done los' his job ah reckon on count of that ere faare which done burned up." I never knew her to speak so broadly as she did yesterday. Reckon that quake shook up her Southern blood.

Left: Twisted steel. Temperatures reached 2000° Fahrenheit.
Bottom: Scene of utter devastation. The Call Building at middle right, in far background.
Both taken from unknown locations.
Darrel Colwell Collection

Rubble mounded in piles in front of a burned out building.
Taken from unknown location. — Darrel Colwell Collection

St. Dunstan's Hotel on Van Ness - dynamited during The Fire.
Gina Janelli Collection

Monday, Day 13 (30th)

Miss Bray came to the store today, and she's as lively as a cricket. Most of the girls are back now, and some of them look scared yet. Been trying to console the poor dears. Helen O'Brien invited me to go with her tomorrow evening to some major's home where she and her folks are stopping and have dinner with them and stay all night and if I go the Lord knows I'll be dead Wednesday, but I guess I'll have to go because there's no way of getting out of it,

Earthquake and Fire damage to an unknown building.
Gina Janelli Collection

and she has been very kind to ask me. It would not be gentlemanly to refuse under the circumstances.

You know we heard at first that it was even worse at Los Angeles than here, and I did not know whether you had been hurt or not. Oakland looks pretty good, and it seemed like old times to be riding on the Key again.

Tuesday, Day 14 (1st May)
I went to the camp with Miss O'Brien.

Crane about to lift load in a clean-up operation.
Taken from an unknown location. — Gina Janelli Collection

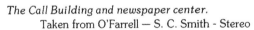

The Call Building and newspaper center.
Taken from O'Farrell — S. C. Smith - Stereo

We had a very nice time. Her folks were very kind to me and made me feel as if I were welcome. We sat around a dandy campfire and all sang including yours truly. I sang There May be Eyes as Brightly Beaming and when I had finished a young lady said to me: "Who is she Mr. Cook?" Helen said: "Oh! his mind is away off from here."

Lovingly, Al

Covering 2,500 acres of The City, ash, rubble, and rain presented a formidable scene. By May, San Francisco was starting to get on its feet. Just two weeks after the total destruction of the business quarter in the downtown area, there began the cleaning out of structures, clearing of foundations, refurbishing and rebuilding, all in a grand effort to restart the financial life of San Francisco. Even the grand Palace Hotel, reduced to its brick walls, with weakened mortar was painstakingly pulled apart and restored using the three million original bricks.

San Francisco was on the rise, and tomorrow would be a better day for San Franciscans who would outlive The Great Earthquake and Fire.

◆

Looking over the Financial District after The Fire.
Taken from Temple Emanu-El toward
Market Street looking southeast.
Stereo View Co. - Stereo

The then 116 year old Mission building remains intact
while the newer church was severely damaged.
Taken from Dolores Street looking west.
Mission Dolores Collection

Ruined building obscuring view of City Hall.
Taken near Market Street looking north. — Edith Irvine photograph; James Irvine Collection

Chapter 5
After The Great Disaster

I've heard some people laugh
And mind you think 'twas witty
As they said, 'tis true indeed
Frisco's now a "Quaker City." — Al Cook

During the two weeks that followed the Earthquake and Fire, San Franciscans showed to the world that they would reclaim their city. If they possibly had not deserved the grand affluence of San Francisco before, they surely had earned it now. This was not because of the disaster and loss, but rather because of their desire to persevere.

Over the course of the next year, all of the services were restored: gas, electricity, telephone, telegraph, water, and trash collection. The transportation system was improved with restoration of cable car service but also with the addition of electric trollies, automobiles, and motorized busses.

Many of the so-called fireproof buildings remained standing and were in fact fireproof. It was their contents and inner framing that was not. The Call, Shreve & Co., the St. Francis, and many other prominent structures were refurbished and operating within the first year or two. The 'Birdcage' Whittle building remained a stark reminder of The Great Disaster for some time, yet it was eventually finished and remains today as do many other buildings predating The Earthquake and Fire.

After The Great Disaster had run its course, city officials and citizens attempted some measure of the losses. There was little good news, but one notable exception was that, contrary to newspaper reports, The City's beloved Cliff House had not tumbled into the Pacific Ocean.

Of some 28,000 buildings that were destroyed, the great majority were lost in The Fire. Fully half The City's population was left homeless, and their dependence on government benefits continued in varying degrees for some

A Critique of Mayor Schmitz and General Funston

The Mayor's response to the temblor was swift, decisive, and generally efficient. He proceeded posthaste to create a Committee of Safety that would guide San Francisco through the emergency and its anticipated aftermath.

Eugene Schmitz formally issued a proclamation instructing that the Gas and Electric Lighting Company immediately and indefinitely suspend services. A curfew was enacted, confining citizens to their residences during the hours of darkness. The proclamation also alerted people to the draconian measures to be taken with those foolish enough to loot or otherwise engage in serious criminal activity.

Some mayoral decisions could, in retrospect, be faulted. In consultation with the Army, Schmitz promoted the use of explosives to make firebreaks, which more often than not spread rather than checked the advancing flames. He authorized the swearing in of private citizens as temporary law enforcers, a mixed blessing. He probably should have allowed citizens more latitude in rescuing possessions and protecting their own homes from the inferno. Some criticism of the relief effort, rightly or wrongly, fell on Schmitz' shoulders.

In any regard, under the circumstances, the Mayor deserved high marks for his coordination of the City's response to calamity, but after the heroic moment was spent, a reform movement was restarted. Indictments and trials followed. In the year following The Earthquake and Fire, Schmitz was found guilty of extortion. His incarceration in the county lockup was brief. His conviction was reversed on appeal. His political boss, Abraham. Ruef, however, received 55 months free room and board at San Quentin.

Emerging from his Russian Hill residence soon after the shocks, General Funston saw fires beginning to burn out of control, and as he proceeded on foot towards Nob Hill he also witnessed firemen hooking up to hydrants lacking water pressure. Grasping immediately the necessity for military participation, Funston commanded both Fort Mason and the Presidio to march all available troops to the Hall of Justice and report to Police Chief Dinan. Less than three hours after the temblor, between 1,500 and 1,700 soldiers were patrolling the downtown area. (There was not that number of firemen and policemen combined in the employ of San Francisco!) The Chief of Police had instructed the soldiers to mete out summary justice to looters and other criminals.

Army regulars were soon dispatched from as far away as the Monterey Presidio and from the Vancouver Barracks in Washington State. The California Militia, the Cadet Corps from the University of California, the Marines, and Navy men all descended on The City.

Funston wired Secretary of War Taft of measures taken by the General and requested the authority to cover those actions. He asked that the War Department send carloads of rations, tents and medicine. By Friday, trains were taking on equipment at Army bases in five states. A well outfitted hospital train was dispatched from Virginia.

For all his personal bombast, Funston knew how to be tactful. He counseled his officers to partner with civilian authorities and bend to their assessments and judgments. If he can be faulted, it would be in regard to his misplaced confidence in the use of explosives to halt The Fire.

When General Greely returned,

(continued on next page)

period of time. Many people, refugees and outsiders alike, found employment rebuilding The City. For two years people came from all over America to help rebuild. Their wages in San Francisco during that time were double what they were elsewhere. So many of those who came to help resurrect The City stayed on in the Bay Area or relocated to Southern California, creating a moderate population boom in the state.

In the period just after The Earthquake and Fire, city boosters began a campaign of downplaying the earthquake and playing up The Fire. Reporters and writers now referred to the disastrous event as "The Great Fire," in order to maximize the money from insurance policies, which payed for fire losses but not for the results of "acts of God" such as earthquakes. It was also a clever strategy to maximize investments.

The Great Disaster arrived seemingly without warning, yet there had been some previous evidence of its coming. No less than 16 tremors had occurred within The City during the previous 12 months — all strong enough to topple shelves, break glass, and be felt up to 200 miles away.

After The Great Fire, the actions of those most responsible for managing the efforts to save San Francisco were assessed. Mayor Schmitz and General Funston were generally applauded for quick thinking and quick action.

Optimistic forecasts for The City's future were published in magazines, newspapers, and books. In the resurgence of The City's business life, photographers marketed thousands of pictures taken of The Fire. Souvenir postcards

Funston relinquished his command. The military presence continued to expand until, several weeks into the occupation, one tenth of the standing Regular Army was bivouacked in The City.

Major General Greely later attempted to give himself more credit than was due his role in The Earthquake and Fire. In this he diminished the role of the Brigadier General, but San Francisco history is more kind to Funston. It also seems to remember the heroics of Schmitz above his shortcomings, and interestingly, the former mayor was later elected to the Board of Supervisors.

Mayor Schmitz Proclamation.
Private Collection

PROCLAMATION BY THE MAYOR

The Federal Troops, the members of the Regular Police Force and all Special Police Officers have been authorized by me to KILL any and all persons found engaged in Looting or in the Commission of Any Other Crime.

I have directed all the Gas and Electric Lighting Co.'s not to turn on Gas or Electricity until I order them to do so. You may therefore expect the city to remain in darkness for an indefinite time.

I request all citizens to remain at home from darkness until daylight every night until order is restored.

I WARN all Citizens of the danger of fire from Damaged or Destroyed Chimneys, Broken or Leaking Gas Pipes or Fixtures, or any like cause.

E. E. SCHMITZ, Mayor

Dated, April 18, 1906.

ALTVATER PRINT, MISSION AND 22D STS.

Magazines

City boosters crafted a climate of optimism to lift the collective spirit of the citizenry and motivate the masses. Their efforts were also directed to the outside world with its potential investors in the city's recovery.

The crucial component to this strategy was the broadcasting of positive information through the popular media. This broad program included communications through artwork, often that gracing the front covers of magazines. These venues frequently drew on mythological and classical imagery to create a symbology for San Francisco's resurrection. Among the more noteworthy examples are two covers of a short lived magazine with the not so subtle name, *The New San Francisco Magazine*, and the covers of the first two post-Earthquake and Fire, *Sunset* magazines.

The first issue of *The New San Francisco Magazine* became the "Salamander Number," so-called for the mythic belief that the amphibian had the ability to emerge from fire unscathed. In the mediaeval lore of alchemy, salamanders were believed to live in fire. The cover of the second issue of *The New California Magazine*, the "Resurrection Number," depicts two animal symbols, the mythical Phoenix and the grizzly bear, which is the animal on the flag of California and on the State Seal. The grizzley is also the official state animal of California. They appear against a backdrop of an emergent San Francisco.

San Francisco painter Maynard Dixon, famous particularly for his bold scenes of the American Southwest, was commissioned by *Sunset* to create cover art for their second May issue, after the first issue was consumed by the fire while in press. The black-and-white cover was an excellent fit to the circumstances. It portrayed a nude woman representing the Spirit of the City, rising skyward from the flaming metropolis. Sophisticated readers, at least, would have recognized the allegorical referent to the fabled male bird of Greek mythology, the phoenix, consumed by fire and reborn from its funeral ashes, but bearing both the personae of the son and of the father.

The *Sunset* that followed, a combined June-July issue, featured another Maynard Dixon cover, one that repeated the optimistic imagery of the May cover; the theme had probably been dictated by the owners of this number one publication in the West, the Southern Pacific Railroad.

More aesthetically pleasing than the May cover, the June-July cover carries the specter of a new city floating above a visual obituary of the old city. Through the ruins stride workers at the ready for rebuilding. The shining white city-to-be is cradled in the arms of an expressionless woman, more apparition than flesh and blood, posed phoenix-like and framed against a backdrop of plumes of smoke, dark at the center but light at the most ascendant margins.

At right: **The Doomed City.**
A number of contemporary books, most hurriedly written, recounted Earthquake and Fire stories in terrifying and macabre terms, often mixed with exaggerated sentiment or pathos. A step above dime novels, accordingly they might cost a quarter. Their often lurid covers telegraphed the genre.
Private Collection

The cover of the June-July 1906 Sunset Magazine.
Private Collection

Covers for the first and second issues of
The New San Francisco Magazine.
Private Collection

The Cliff House

Among the varied false information bandied about, whether by word of mouth rumor or by errant newspaper accounts, one of the most preposterous stories concerned the Cliff House that sat on solid rock at ocean's edge. The April 18 first edition *Oakland Enquirer* blared "Cliff House Topples into the Ocean." In fact, the restaurant and hotel had not been "thrown from its foundation," but rather remained undamaged by either temblor or fire. Other Enquirer reportage was reasonably accurate, a function of the inverse relationship that exists between level of news accuracy and distance from events. Had Pulitzer established a category for prescience, certainly the Enquirer qualified, as this Cliff House built in 1896 was destroyed in 1907, but by fire not quake. The owner of the third Cliff House was Adolph Sutro who had made millions from the Comstock in Nevada. Sutro's mansion sat on a crag overlooking the restaurant and hotel.

depicted the fallen Valencia Hotel, scenes of damaged churches, and so on. Cheap novels further sensationalized what was already quite sensational. A great many books with myriad images of devastation sold well.

Just one year and a day after The Earthquake, Al Cook and Mabel Moody were married. Al stayed on for a time at Pacific Hardware and Steel. Al and Mabel later adopted a daughter.

One hundred years after The City's tragedy there are continued observances of both The Earthquake and Fire. One is a gathering at Lotta's Fountain, and includes '06 survivors. Another ceremonial get-together is at the only fire hydrant that continued to supply precious water when all other hydrants failed. It is located in Al Cook's old neighborhood.

◆

View of Cliff House, 1906 or 1907.
Keystone View Company - Stereo

The famous gold fire hydrant at the corner of 20th and Church streets.
Private Collection

Top: *Mabel on her wedding day.*
Bottom: *Wedding invitation of Al and Mabel.*

Mr. and Mrs. John H. Moody
announce the marriage of their daughter
Mabel
to
Mr. John Alphonso Cook
on Saturday, the twentieth of April
in the year one thousand nine hundred and seven
Oakland, California

Al and Mabel Cook

Al Cook and Mabel Moody were married on April 20, 1907, in Oakland, one year after the San Francisco Earthquake and Fire. After, the Pacific Hardware and Steel Company transferred Al to Portland where he managed a Sporting Goods Department. In 1917, he returned to Pacific Hardware in San Francisco, and he and Mabel adopted newborn Barbara Jean, their only child.

Subsequently, he took a position as Special Representative of the Remington Arms Union Metallic Cartridge Company in Seattle. By that time he had been for several years one of the best known outdoor sportsmen on the West Coast. He was a champion trapshooter who loved hunting and fishing.

Next, he became a partner in a small business, the Kimball Gun Store in Tacoma, but when the partnership went sour, he was welcomed back by Remington in 1920, this time to head up their Portland office. Al Cook died unexpectedly at age 40 in Portland (1921) from an overdose of anesthetic while undergoing an appendectomy.

Now a widow, Mabel moved to the East Bay. She was soon working out of her home. The business, "Mabel Moody Cook's Cakes," at one time counted a clientele of about 1000. She retired before the end of the Depression.

In the following years, Mabel Cook watched her daughter's family grow, playing the role of kindly, indulgent grandmother to a boy and two girls. She married again at age 69, to Benjamin Franklin Edwards, and was widowed a second time, in 1968, after twenty-one and a half years of marriage. In 1976, Mabel passed away in Sonoma, California.

Al Cook

Index

Al Cook's Letters & Postcards

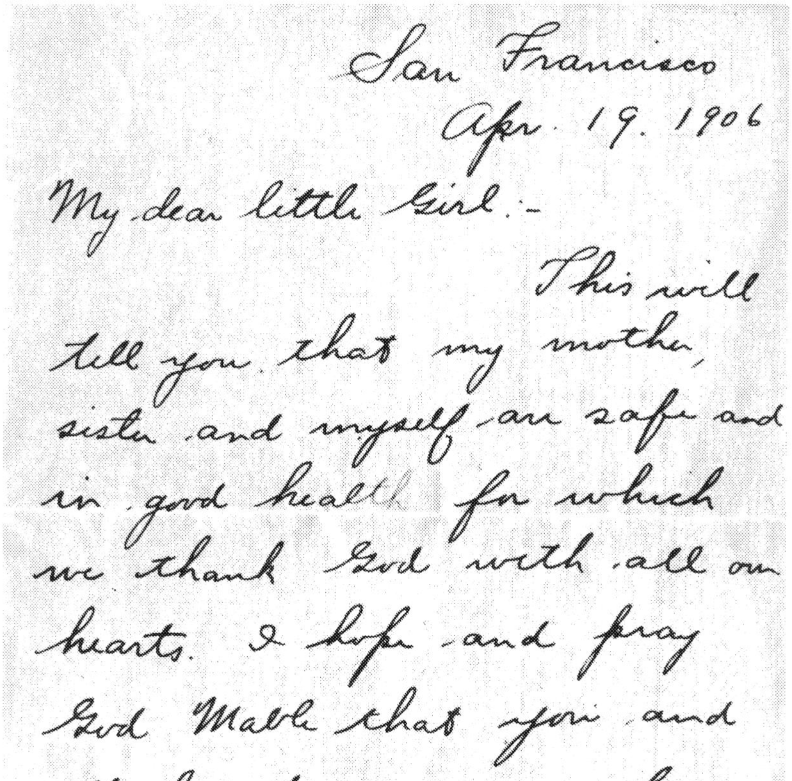

San Francisco
Apr. 19. 1906

My dear little Girl:—

This will
tell you that my mother,
sister and myself are safe and
in good health for which
we thank God with all our
hearts. I hope and pray
God Mable that you and
all dear to you are safe
also.

You cannot emagine the
suffering which has been

caused by the temblor. People are dead by the score and on top of it all the whole city is slowly burning up. The water mains are broken and in consequence there is little or no water with which to fight the fire

The whole down town district is in ruins from Valencia St to the bay and the fire is now raging on Powell St Hill on that side and is now burning the Fairmont and Hopkins. Every thing on the Hill is gone. The St Francis went about 2 this morning. The Call burned yesterday noon. Can you imagine it? The city is nothing but ruins.

We are at this time very uncertain as to how long we will be able to stay in our home as the fire is burning at 17 th & Howard and 14 th & Valencia

We are living in a tent on
the hill as are hundreds
of familys who were burned
out

The town is under
martial law and the soldiers
are taking all provisions and
dealing them out evenly to
those who most need them.
The suffering is terrible.
Elsie will probably be burned
out in about 2 hours unless
they are to check the fire.
They are blowing up buildings

in the path of the fire and in that way they are able to control it - sometimes.

The sight of the burning city is truly grand yet it is awful when you think of the loss of property and life. I do not know what we will do. There is no place to buy things and they will not allow a fire to be built in any house. People are cooking on camp stoves, and one fires of any description. We are fixed fine as we have a dandy tent and a fine camp stove. Had fried eggs and flap jacks for breakfast. Fine shooting

The P H & S Co is not burned and we will resume work in a few days. It is the only store of any size left in the city. Some of the outside walls were shaken down and the two tanks went through the building from roof to basement. The

buildings were not otherwise damaged;
for which I am very thankful as we
will have a place to work. I am
going to guard the store to-night and
I am writing this before I go to sleep.

Yesterday morning just after the
shock I went down to Valencia st
and worked for 2 and ½ hours on the
Valencia st Hotel. The Hotel was a
4 story frame building and went
down in a heap burying about 100

people. The earth is split open and on Valencia St it has sunk about 10 ft. Stores on Valencia are all knocked topsy-turvy and in a great many cases you cannot see them at all as they have sunk out of sight. Just think the tracks on Valencia St are like the letter "S". The whole st is twisted.

As I was saying I worked on the Valencia St Hotel and we chopped out dozens of people some dead and some alive. I had the pleasure of saving one whole family, a mother & father and a little girl baby. I was poking around with my ax and calling and I heard the women answer. I chopped through the wreckage and after some hard work managed to locate them. The mother called to save her child and as luck would have it I soon had the little one safe and sound. The dear little baby was nursing a rubber nipple and was not even scratched. The mother was not hurt and it was worth any amount of labor to see the joy of that mother at having her baby restored to her safe and sound. The man was held down by a plank which was across his foot but he was not badly injured. The only thing that saved them was that they slept in iron bedsteads.

Went down to the store this morning and I pray God I may never see such wreck, and ruin again. Why Mabel people are lying dead in the streets burned to a crisp. The suffering amongst the poor class who lived in that district will be terrible as in a great many cases all they saved was the clothes they wore.

The soldiers have shot several thieves yet I dare say there is any amount of robbery going on.

The city hall is a perfect wreck

and they released all the prisoners
yesterday morning. There were
400 of them.

Have just been to look
at the fire again. It is a
regular Hell on earth. I do
not know whether they can stop
it or not. The breeze is
fanning it and it is traveling
like wild.

We are packing up our
things and will be ready to
leave as soon as necessary.
Our home was not damaged

and our water has been running all the time.

Guess I'll have to close now so will say good-bye and will pray for you whom I wish I could see now and hope you will pray for us. May God's mercy and protection ever be near and keep you Mable untill we are able to meet again.

Lovingly,

al

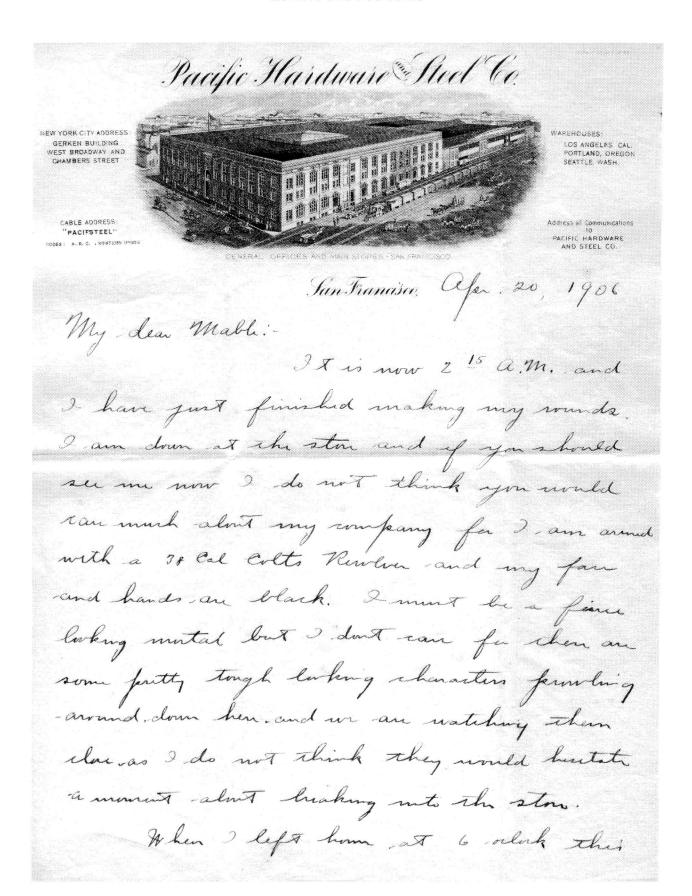

Pacific Hardware Steel Co.

NEW YORK CITY ADDRESS:
GERKEN BUILDING
WEST BROADWAY AND
CHAMBERS STREET

WAREHOUSES:
LOS ANGELES, CAL.
PORTLAND, OREGON
SEATTLE, WASH.

CABLE ADDRESS:
"PACIFSTEEL"
CODES: A. B. C. , WESTERN UNION

Address all Communications
to
PACIFIC HARDWARE
AND STEEL CO.

GENERAL OFFICES AND MAIN STORES - SAN FRANCISCO

San Francisco, Apr. 20, 1906

My dear Mable:—

It is now 2¹⁵ A.M. and I have just finished making my rounds. I am down at the store and if you should see me now I do not think you would care much about my company for I am armed with a 38 Cal Colts Revolver and my face and hands are black. I must be a fierce looking mortal but I dont care for there are some pretty tough looking characters prowling around down here and we are watching them close as I do not think they would hesitate a moment about breaking into the store.

When I left home at 6 oclock this

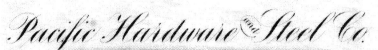

San Francisco,

evening the fire had not reached us yet
but was very near. The College of Notre Dame
which is as you know just across from the
Mission Dolores was one mass of flames when
I left. We have all our things on the hills
where they will be safe.

Have just taken another walk and
a fireman told me that the fire had been
stopped at 20th St so else I guess is
safe. He did not know how far up the
valley the fire had burnt so I do not know
whether our home was burnt or not.

There are people camping just across from
the store in the railroad yards and their con—

Pacific Hardware and Steel Co.

NEW YORK CITY ADDRESS:
GERKEN BUILDING
WEST BROADWAY AND
CHAMBERS STREET

CABLE ADDRESS:
"PACIFSTEEL"
CODES: A. B. C. - WESTERN UNION

GENERAL OFFICES AND MAIN STORES - SAN FRANCISCO

WAREHOUSES:
LOS ANGELES, CAL.
PORTLAND, OREGON
SEATTLE, WASH.

Address all Communications
to
PACIFIC HARDWARE
AND STEEL CO.

San Francisco,

dition is serious. They have no food and are getting desperate. They look at you with angry looks (that is the men) and I really think that the only thing which keeps them from attacking us is the fact that we are fully armed.

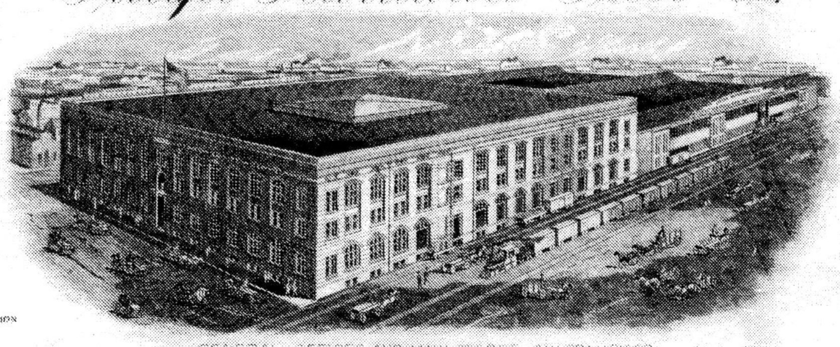

Roasted bodies are numerous in this locality. They are in most cases on the sidewalks and are mostly men who were probably drunk and could not get away.

Must close now Mable girl and untill I hear from you I shall be anxious

Your cop ✧

Al

Scottish Rite Temple and New Synagogue. Postmarked May 8, 1906.

St. Dominic's Church. Postmarked May 8, 1906.

Valencia Street Hotel Postmarked April 9, 1908. Sent to Mrs. J.A. Cook (Mabel Moody).

City Hall. Postmarked May 3, 1906.

Stereoscopic Views

**Full Size Stereo Views of
San Francisco's 1906 Earthquake and Fire**

Looking northeast from Twin Peaks down Market Street
to the Ferry Building. San Francisco, Calif.

Looking South, from the corner of Sutter and Stockton.

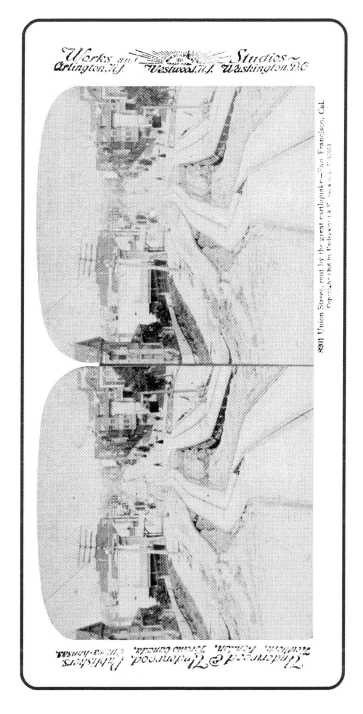

Union Street, rent by the great earthquake - San Francisco, Cal.

Postoffice Entrance on Mission Street.

Refugees camping front of ferry.

The Ferry Building from Market & Stewart
showing the sunken street.

The Call Building in a maelstrom of flame - The Great San Francisco Fire - completing the devastation of the famous Spreckels' structure.

Horrors of the earthquake and fire - near Union Square looking east toward the Call Building; San Francisco.

Up Telegraph Hill in the Wake of the Earthquake and Fire - San Francisco Disaster of April 18, 1906.

Refugees' camp on Telegraph Hill; San Francisco, Cal.

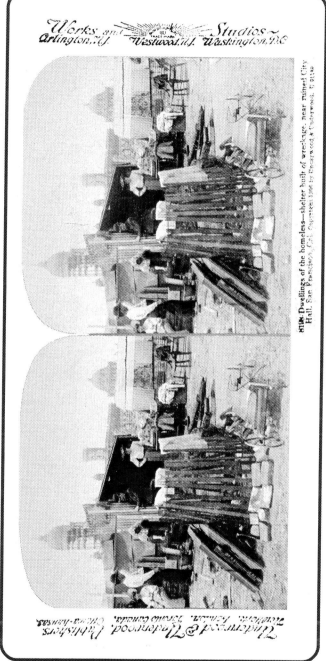

The Crocker residence and wrecked automobiles, ruined by Earthquake and Fire; San Francisco, Cal.

Dwellings of the homeless - shelter built of wreckage near the ruined City Hall; San Francisco, Cal.

One of the sights which Beggears description - Telegraph Hill, looking east from Union and Leavenworth streets.

Ruins of the Emma Spreckels Building, San Francisco Earthquake Disaster, 1906.

Looking northwest from the corner of Ellis and Powell streets.

Hall of Justice with tower shaken down by the great earthquake; San Francisco, Cal.

Some of the first street car service after the great fire;
San Francisco, Cal.

Men working in the rubble, SE From Montgomery &
Vallejo streets.

California Street looking toward the ferry depot - Banking District.

City Hall - Photographer in foreground - Tall brick chimneys left standing.

Looking up Grant Avenue from Market Street.

Valencia Street, which sank four feet breaking a great water main; San Francisco Disaster.

Curious result of the earthquake - settling of houses on
Howard Street; San Francisco Disaster.

Looking from Portsmouth Square at the ruined city;
San Francisco, California.

Washington Street in Chinatown, looking east from Stockton Street.

Nob Hill and the Fairmont Hotel; Chinatown in the foreground; San Francisco Disaster.

View of Nob Hill, the millionaire residence district.

Grace Episcopal Church and surroundings.

Burning of San Francisco, looking toward the Bay from Nob Hill; all seen was subsequently burned.

True grit - Barber painting sign on tent stretched on sidewalk of former place.

Bank safes being guarded.

Refugees' camp at ball grounds in Golden Gate Park.

Forming bread line at Jefferson Square.

From Moulder School distributing station, showing tons of flour on sidewalk.

*The Call Building and Newspaper Center from
O'Farrell Street, San Francisco.*

The Call Building, from Bush & Powell Street.

Cliff House and Seal Rocks, San Francisco, Calif.

City Hall from McAllister Street, looking northeast - Souvenir hunters in foreground.

*Looking east from corner of Pine and Stockton,
showing the ruins of the Mills building.*

*Refugees' camp, former dwelling in ruins in
background. This is earthquake work.*

*The City Hall shaken into ruins by the Earthquake;
San Francisco, April 1906.*

*Curious wreck of the Steiner Street Catholic Church
and settled houses; San Francisco Disaster.*

Ruins of the Jewish Synagogue; San Francisco.

Looking east from the corner of Ellis and Jones streets.

Refugee camp made of scrap iron.

Seventh Regiment of the National Guards, from Los Angeles.

Ruins of St. Ignatius Catholic Church.

Looking west from the Jewish Synagogue.

Ruins of the Jewish Synagogue on Sutter St.

Refugees' camp in Jefferson Square.

Gathering a few home relics at the ruins of the Wenban Palace, Van Ness Ave., San Francisco.

From Telegraph Hill southeast past the Ferry Building; the tower to the Union Iron Works and docks; San Francisco.

The Phil B. Bekeart Co., Inc. formerly at
114 Second St. San Francisco, moved to Alameda.
Granddaugher Laura Bekeart Dietz

Colophon

Morris Fuller Benton designed Souvenir in 1914, drawing from his earlier Antiqua and Kursiv typestyles he did at the Schelter & Giesecke foundry. Ed Benquiat drew the International Typeface Corporation version used here, in 1970. Souvenir is informal and rounded in appearance, and it creates an open and nostalgic feeling. It is frequently found in college publications and in the advertising industry.

Templar, a victorian era typestyle, is used in the title and chapter heads.